The Alexander Technique Birth Book

לספרי המרכבה

אילן

אוקטובר 1993

The Alexander Technique Birth Book

A Guide to Better Pregnancy, Natural
Childbirth and Parenthood

Ilana Machover and Angela and
Jonathan Drake

Robinson
LONDON

Robinson Publishing Ltd
7, Kensington Church Court
London W8 4SP

First published by Robinson Publishing Ltd 1993

Photography for cover and chapters 2, 3, 4, 5 and 6 by
Julian Easten, other photography (on pp. 130, 141, 142 and 147) by
authors.
Illustrations by Helen Chown.

A copy of the British Library Cataloguing in Publication
Data for this title is available from the British Library.

ISBN 1–85487–186–2

Typeset by Textype Typesetters, Cambridge
Printed by Bath Press in England

Contents

About the Authors

Ilana Machover is a qualified teacher of the Alexander Technique and Medau Rhythmic Movement, and an advanced teacher for Britain's National Childbirth Trust. She assists at Misha Magidov's training school for Alexander teachers. As part of her private practice, she runs special courses for pregnant women. She has also given many workshops for midwives, antenatal (prenatal) teachers and Alexander teachers, on the relevance of the Technique to childbirth. She has two children and three grandchildren.

Angela and **Jonathan Drake** have three children between them – two born at home, one in hospital assisted by a community midwife. Angela first had lessons in the Alexander Technique in 1985. It has proved invaluable during her recent pregnancy and in the birth of their youngest child, and helps her cope with the demands of family life! Her main involvement with the book was in editing the text. Jonathan, a medical graduate, worked in health education for a number of years before qualifying as a teacher of the Alexander Technique in 1982. He is the author of *Body Know-How: A practical guide to the use of the Alexander Technique in everyday life* (1991) and *Thorsons Introductory Guide to the Alexander Technique* (1993). He also teaches t'ai chi and is a consultant on ergonomic problems in the workplace.

Acknowledgements

Ilana's contribution to this book grew out of many years of work with pregnant women. I am grateful to the National Childbirth Trust (NCT) for training me and for its continual contribution to my development as a childbirth educator. I am also grateful to the women and their partners who attended my NCT classes, and to all who participated in my *Eutokia* (Greek for 'good birth') Alexander classes for pregnant women. Special thanks are due to those who wrote to me after the birth of their children and allowed me to quote from their letters. I would like to thank my colleagues in the North-West London branch of the NCT, and the many Alexander teachers with whom I have had fruitful discussions.

I owe a great debt to my teacher of the Alexander Technique, Misha Magidov, for his inspiring teaching as well as for his encouragement and support.

Jane Armstrong, Sally Burger, Brigitte Cavadias, Juliet Faradon, Helen Lewison and Gill Wilkinson read the manuscript of Chapters 2, 3 and 4, made useful comments and offered much encouragement. Patricia Donnithorne, Librarian of the NCT, provided expert bibliographic assistance.

My greatest debt is to my husband Moshé, for his help and love.

I would like to dedicate this book to my grandchildren Naomi, Sacha and Eli, whose births reinforced my commitment to the ideas expressed in it.

Angela and **Jonathan** are indebted to Linda Gillard, whose initial enthusiasm for a project of this kind contributed to its genesis. Chapter 6 took shape with the help of her comments, and Esmé Glauert also made many useful suggestions. We are also grateful to the following for permission to quote at length: Adam Nott, editor of the *Alexander Journal*, Joyce Warrack's report on Irene Tasker's work at Alexander's 'little school'; and Jean Shepherd, from her account of her Alexander–based remedial reading project. Finally, the heart of Chapter 6 is in the moving stories generously provided by Ann Mathews from her unpublished Master's thesis.

And, not least, we are grateful to our children, Mika, Leead and Matthew, for their forbearance during the writing of this book and especially during its 'transitional stage'!

All three of us are extremely grateful to Karoline Feuerbach for allowing us to include her account of the birth of her two daughters – a major contribution to this book.

We also thank Helen Chown, artist, for her skill and patience; Julian Easten for his excellent photography; Penelope Easten and Annie Girling for their demonstrations. Finally, thanks are due to our editors at Robinson Publishing, Annabel Edwards and Caroline Black.

Ilana was largely responsible for Chapters 2–4, Angela and Jonathan for Chapters 1, 5 and 6. Notwithstanding all the assistance we have received with the manuscript, we are, of course, entirely responsible for any errors that may remain.

Foreword

Our first son, Sam, was born at home and we were planning another home birth for our second child.

When we were expecting Sam we attended a National Childbirth Trust antenatal class. But as seven years had passed since then, we felt we needed some kind of refresher course. We had a few sessions with Ilana, who applies the Alexander Technique in her antenatal teaching. As actors, we had of course heard about the Technique as a means of improving performance through good use of the body; but we were intrigued as to how it might be applied to childbirth. In the event, it all made very good sense.

Now, several years later, we still remember that giving ourselves Alexander Technique directions and consciously releasing tension, while staying upright or on all fours, helped us to cope with the pain and made the course of labour smoother. Ilana's enthusiasm and belief in natural childbirth also helped in bolstering our confidence. It all went well; Jeremy played a very active supporting role, and we both found that we had unexpected reserves of energy to draw on. In the early morning, our son Max was born with great ease.

We are delighted to see that Ilana, Angela and Jonathan have written this book, which explains the application of the Alexander Technique to childbirth and parenthood. Looking after babies and young children is physically demanding, and good use of one's body can help in dealing better with both the joys and the stresses involved.

We hope this book will help many other parents to experience a natural and happy childbirth.

Sinead Cusack
Jeremy Irons

Introduction

This is a guide to how women and their partners can use the Alexander Technique to help prepare for the special demands of pregnancy, childbirth and parenthood.

When a woman is pregnant, she looks inwards to gather her energies for the profound changes in her life that will follow. The Alexander Technique – which teaches improved coordination and mind–body functioning – can not only be a rich and powerful method of self-help at this time, but is also a resource to be tapped for the whole of our lives.

We hope to fill a gap in pre- or antenatal education by applying the educational ideas of F.M. Alexander to childbirth. They have important implications for women's health and well-being and for optimal foetal development. Many of the health problems brought on by childbearing can be traced back to faulty posture and poor patterns of body use developing over previous years; these problems may become intractable unless new ways of being and moving are learnt. Back pain, for example, is often a direct consequence of gradually adopting a more exaggerated sway-back posture to cope with the weight of the rapidly growing baby.

How does the Alexander Technique work? You become more aware of faulty patterns of body use that have overlaid the natural poise and ease of movement which is our birthright, and it enables you to 'undo' them. Concerned less with specific movements (although certain suggestions will be made), it is essentially to do with *a certain quality of mind and body use which can inform all our activities.* You are encouraged to give more attention to *how* you perform even the simplest of daily tasks; in little ways at first, then in more complex activities, you find yourself moving with greater facility, and with less strain and waste of energy.

Your body becomes a more sensitive instrument through which you can adapt more effectively to change. This is of special importance during pregnancy; and during the heightened drama of birth itself, the Alexander Technique gives you more control over your reactions to the pain of

1

contractions. It helps you to 'get out of the way' of the powerful forces of labour – promoting natural childbirth – and therefore reducing the need for medical intervention.

In the final chapters, we shall discuss the relevance of the Alexander Technique to the early months after birth, to parenthood and education; how to cope more effectively with the demands of feeding and lifting and carrying your baby; and the extra chores that having children inevitably brings. And what is the best way to get back into shape? The fourteen-day quick-fix exercise plan may do more harm than good. Our body sense can be – and commonly is – a disconcertingly unreliable guide to maintaining good body use in our daily activities. Exercise routines, even undertaken with the best of intentions to improve well-being and fitness, carry the danger of hastening decline in our coordination and functioning.

As parents, we want to foster the full potential of our children. One of the delights of toddlers is to observe their almost tireless ease and freedom of movement. Marked deterioration, though, usually sets in by later childhood, but it doesn't have to be so: as parents and teachers, we have a duty to prevent this as far as we can, and some of the main pitfalls will be indicated.

We have not tried to make this book a comprehensive primer on obstetrics, nor can it be a substitute for the experience of individual work as a basis for learning the Technique. We hope it inspires you to take lessons from a qualified teacher, that it supports you in that experience and that it will help you in your self-development and that of your family. And, whatever antenatal classes you decide to attend, we hope that you will find this book a valuable guide. Alexander's basic discoveries are of great significance to humankind – all the more so when the quickening pace of technological advance seems out of step with our personal development.

Note: To avoid the clumsiness of he/she, we refer to the Alexander teacher as female, a birth partner as male, the unborn baby as neutral and the child as male.

1

Why the Alexander Technique?

As a medical student in the early 1970s, Jonathan had the temerity to suggest to a consultant obstetrician that natural childbirth might have certain virtues. The woman they had both just seen at her pre- or antenatal check-up had wanted the birth of her child to be an ecstatic experience – 'like having ten thousand orgasms', she said. It didn't turn out at all as she had imagined: the baby was in a posterior presentation, making labour long and painful. She lay back on the hospital bed bemused by the pain of it all, was persuaded to have an epidural anaesthetic and was finally delivered of her baby by Caesarean section. She felt cheated of giving birth.

Today, many pregnant women in the West enjoy tremendous advantages: the general level of health is much higher than that of previous generations or indeed of our contemporaries in the rest of the world. Thanks to improved standards of living, as well as advances in hygiene and preventive medicine, mothers and babies are healthier: both neonatal mortality and maternal deaths have been dramatically reduced. But such progress has also brought with it the tendency to over-medicalize the normal transitions of life, including pregnancy and childbirth.

1990 marked the centenary of the birth of Grantly Dick Read, pioneer of the natural birth movement. Despite his influence and that of many who have come after him, the general situation in obstetrics and midwifery is still very much as described by Dr Marsden Wagner, writing in that same year:

> We take a young, impressionable woman who is pregnant and put her into a system which defines pregnancy as a disease. Much of what we do to her during her pregnancy gives her the message that she is not capable of being pregnant and having a baby without professional help. By the time the birth comes she is feeling inadequate. Then what happens at birth? She gets the message that she couldn't give birth to a baby without professional help. The monitors, induction, all of these say to her: your

3

body is not enough, is it? . . . We define pregnancy as a disease, birth as a surgical procedure . . . This is what I call disabling help.[1]

Preparation for Birth

What preparation is necessary for women to give birth unhindered and with minimal medical intervention? We believe that, of all psycho-physical methods currently known, the Alexander Technique has the most to contribute to healthier pregnancy and natural childbirth. It has the practical knowledge of how we move and coordinate ourselves and respond to stress, which would enable women – aided by a favourable environment – to give birth in the easiest and most natural way. Women hope to have short, pain-free labour and yet, even with extensive experience of the Alexander Technique (as you will see in Karoline's story at the end of Chapter 4), expectations about the outcome need to be realistic. Each birth is a powerful experience of the unknown and cannot be exactly predetermined.

In this chapter, we shall take an overview of some of the most influential methods of preparing for birth. We shall then introduce the Alexander Technique and describe its particular relevance to pregnancy and childbirth. Preparation for birth, as you will see, is largely about learning to cooperate with what is, in essence, an extraordinarily powerful, involuntary process. This involves being able to exercise what Alexander called *conscious control* in order to prevent ourselves falling back into habitual ways of dealing with stressful situations – especially pain – by increasing tension. The better your body use and stress management skills in your everyday activities – which the Alexander Technique can help you improve – the easier you will find it to *give* birth with confidence.

A Brief History of Childbirth

At one time, in the Western world, a woman giving birth would have been assisted by the local midwife at home, often using a birth stool to facilitate an upright position. In the seventeenth century in France the use of obstetric forceps was developed and it soon became fashionable for the upper classes to be 'confined' to bed for the birth in what has come to be described as the 'stranded beetle' position. This made it easier for their medical attendants to take charge and to see what they were doing when medical intervention became necessary – as it frequently did (most of the conditions for a natural birth having been denied). Over the next three hundred years there were further surgical advances and developments in anaesthesia and analgesia (pain relief).

Medical management of birth
By the 1970s, 'active management of labour' had become the norm:

labour was routinely induced and the membrane (the bag of fluid surrounding the foetus) artificially ruptured. This procedure can cause foetal distress; a vicious circle was often set in motion, creating the need for further intervention and producing unwanted effects on mother and baby. The foetus was electronically monitored for any sign of distress, thereby limiting the woman's movements and ironically often creating the very problem it was supposed to probe; episiotomy (cutting the perineum) was often carried out in order to speed the delivery of the baby. Drugs for pain relief usually became necessary to make the artificially driven contractions bearable. This had the effect of damping down sensitivity to the body's signals, undermining the woman's capacity to respond actively and to give birth unaided; and the drugs given zonked the baby (interfering with bonding between mother and baby). An epidural (spinal anaesthetic), if given, was frequently followed by a forceps delivery. And all the while food was denied in case of the need for a general anaesthetic.

Perhaps the most disturbing fact about routine 'active management of labour' was that it was not subjected to proper scientific trials to find out whether, on balance, it would be of benefit to the majority of women and their babies. Obstetricians had the technology and their (apparent) success in its use added kudos to what had traditionally been regarded as a low-status surgical speciality. Doctors inducing labour ('we'll get her cracking along') needed to intervene all the way down the line as normal physiology was subverted. As a result, natural, normal, physiological birth became less common and did not *appear* to be wanted by most women.

Grass-roots challenge
How did this move to medical management come about? Our culture encourages passivity and dependency in women and it is tempting to hand over responsibility for ourselves to the 'experts'. Deeply buried fears about pain and mortality can be stirred up by the experience of pregnancy and childbirth. It may well seem easier to have someone else manage the event for us, to take away pain and persuade us that it must be safer for the baby. In addition, medical attendants may undermine a woman's confidence in her own ability to give birth. In labour she is vulnerable and more easily intimidated. For example: 'you are only 2 cm dilated'; 'unless you have such and such a procedure you will put your baby at risk', or the repeated exhortation 'push, push, *push!*' unrelated to the woman's own body messages and rhythm of contractions or to any real need to do so.

Although there are obviously situations where medical intervention is necessary, routine active management of labour has not been justified. In the last twenty years, evidence for the capacity of women to give birth to their babies naturally and with minimal intervention has mounted and is now overwhelming. In addition, there is greater understanding of the incredible intricacy of the hormonal and other regulatory mechanisms of labour, and their effectiveness and efficiency in delivering most babies safely, if not disturbed.

Paradoxically, the period of greatest development of technology in childbirth – the late 1960s and 1970s – coincided with the rise of the women's liberation movement, when women became more aware of their needs and began to fight for control over their lives, including the processes of pregnancy and birth.

Natural childbirth pioneers: The beginnings of change

The English general practitioner Grantly Dick Read put the case for natural childbirth, first in a book in the 1930s, and then in his 1944 classic *Childbirth Without Fear*. He described a turning point, early in his career, when a young woman who had refused his offer of anaesthesia commented after her easy birth, 'It didn't hurt. It wasn't meant to, was it, doctor?' Until then he had believed that severe pain was an inevitable part of the childbirth process.

As he observed the fear and pain of many women in childbirth over subsequent months, he began to question whether this would be the normal course of events if women were better prepared for birth. His main insight was that fear, tension and pain are interlinked and that if they hold sway during labour, birth will be made much more problematic. He came to believe that women would be less fearful if they knew more about labour and birth and he therefore began antenatal education. As well as teaching the relevant information about pregnancy and birth, this consisted of various exercises: relaxation and toning, initially; breathing techniques were added later.

Apart from reservations that are raised by the Alexander Technique, about the whole notion of doing exercises, most natural childbirth advocates nowadays would firmly reject Alexander's insistence on women lying down in the first stage of labour! That being said, the great achievement of this early pioneer was his vision of birth as a *physiological*, rather than *pathological* process, and the fact that he listened to – and heard in the main – women's experiences of themselves in labour.

About the same time, the French obstetrician Fernand Lamaze was developing what he called a 'psycho-prophylactic' approach, based on mental control to prevent problems in labour. This was to become, undoubtedly, the most influential method of antenatal education. Lamaze's assumption seemed to be that women couldn't possibly *know how* to give birth: they had to be taught, in the same way that you learn how to swim or write or read. His original approach involved women learning – in a lying-down position – special patterns of breathing for different stages of labour. In this way – and reminded if necessary by their partners – women in labour were supposed to be able to distance themselves from any pain. It is not clear how this dissociation from the body could be effective if labour was prolonged (as it might well be in the recumbent position). If it appeared to be failing, anxiety about losing control would be likely to inhibit the natural progress of labour.

The British scene

The National Childbirth Trust (NCT), which has become well known throughout Britain for its advocacy of natural childbirth and its classes for expectant parents, was started in 1955 as an association for the 'promotion and better understanding of the Dick Read system'. Gradually other methods and ideas were incorporated, particularly those of Lamaze and Sheila Kitzinger. Erna Wright, one of the first childbirth educators in the UK, visited France in 1960 and was introduced to Lamaze's method of psycho-prophylaxis.

Sheila Kitzinger, a social anthropologist, had worked independently before she became aware of the NCT's existence. She joined it in the early 1960s. Her influence was decisive, due to her fighting spirit and determined questioning of authority. Her approach includes aspects of both the Dick Read and Lamaze methods and incorporates the idea of active birth movements and positions. At the same time, she prefers to 'focus on birth as experience rather than a series of exercises in breathing and relaxation'. Her extensive writings on the emotional and psycho-sexual aspects of childbirth have influenced and empowered women around the world.

The French connection

The tide in favour of more natural birth had begun to gather momentum with the publication of Frederick Leboyer's *Birth Without Violence* in the mid-1970s. Leboyer brought the skills of an obstetrician and a poet's sensibility to enquire into the nature of the experience of birth for the *baby*. The newborn should not, he said, have its senses assaulted by bright lights, noise from insensitive birth attendants and harsh touch. He recommended delay in cutting the cord and stressed the value of easing the transition from the womb to the outside world by placing the newborn baby in a warm bath for a little while.

Perhaps the most important single contribution of all from the medical profession, following on from Leboyer, has been made by Michel Odent. Whereas Leboyer had pointed the way to the necessary conditions for a gentle birth for the baby, Odent focused on the *woman's* needs in labour. Working as a general surgeon in a busy local hospital in Pithiviers, France, he was often required to perform Caesarean sections as there was no resident obstetrician. Because this took a great deal of his scarce time, he began to wonder what was happening that seemed to require so much intervention. So he began afresh to observe women in labour, endeavouring to respond to their needs. In this way, he was able to clarify a number of conditions that seemed necessary for labour to proceed normally; and he created an 'ideal' environment in his hospital for women to give birth spontaneously, without pain relief, and with fewer complications than occur in most obstetric units. The best environment for birth, he claimed, is essentially that in which most couples would choose to make love. He called the birthing room a *salle sauvage* (a 'natural' room) – a place quite unlike the delivery room of most hospitals, more like a bedroom furnished with a large low platform and cushions – where the woman in labour can feel free to be herself and adopt whatever positions seem right to her.

Odent acknowledges his debt to Leboyer in stressing the importance of subdued lighting, quiet and warmth, and care in not disturbing the contact between mother and child. Pithiviers was renowned for not offering pain killers and for the provision of pools of warm water, primarily for relaxation, but also where underwater births occasionally happened; and because many women gave birth in a supported squatting position. However the main feature, he says (in *Birth Re-born: What Birth Can and Should be*), should be the attitude of the midwife who stays with the woman throughout her labour: 'a belief in the instinctive potential of human beings and in the innate knowledge women bring to childbirth'. This certainly could be felt in the atmosphere of the place, with the calm, unhurried, unforced demeanour of the staff.

The Pithiviers hospital served a local rural community and, while Odent worked there, it attracted people from far and wide. Many women – often those fearing an otherwise complicated birth or those who had been threatened with intervention – made the pilgrimage to have their babies in Odent's unit. For others, a visit boosted their confidence *within themselves* – if not at home, perhaps with a community midwife in their local hospital – that would enable them to achieve a better birth.

Remarkably, the results justified every claim that Odent made: measures of outcome at Pithiviers showed a substantially lower incidence of maternal and neonatal complications than is obtained in most obstetric units.

The need for a 'holistic' approach

Although F.M. Alexander was at the height of his career at about the same time as Dick Read and Lamaze, it is curious that there was no contact between them. It is not generally known that Alexander had an interest in the effect of faulty body coordination on pregnancy and birth. In his last book he quotes from *Body Mechanics*, written by a group of orthopaedic surgeons:

> Much of the gynaecological disability and long periods of weakness following some pregnancies can be explained on the basis that the compensation for long-standing faulty body mechanics has been broken by the burden of pregnancy and parturition, and when once broken, the badly used body is unable to regain its compensation and strength. A proper understanding of the correction of faulty body mechanics would avoid much of this trouble.[2]

To our knowledge, the method that comes closest to encouraging improved 'body mechanics' and the flexibility of response necessary for a better pregnancy and childbirth is the Alexander Technique. It is not, of course, a panacea. As with any method, it cannot be successfully 'grafted' on late in pregnancy and be expected to make all the difference to the outcome of labour. It will be effective in so far as it is applied but it alone cannot guarantee that childbirth will be entirely natural. Every woman has her own attitudes and beliefs and particular ways of moving, and a previous medical history; and there are other factors to be considered, such as genetic make-up, nutrition and the approach of medical staff. The earlier in pregnancy, therefore, that you are introduced to Alexander's principles, the more you can benefit. Best of all is to have lessons for some time beforehand so that it becomes an important part of you.

Why do we claim that the Alexander Technique takes a truly holistic approach? There are a number of reasons. First, it has a clear vision of the whole person – a psycho-physical self – as you will see shortly; and it is an approach based on not trying to deal directly with *symptoms* so much as *seeking to improve functioning as a whole*. It is concerned with how we respond to stress and how we can actually thrive on stress. It is not just something to be practised in special circumstances in the hope that it will stay with us when we are under pressure but, rather, it offers fundamental practical knowledge for living life from moment to moment. It provides a clear model of how we should coordinate ourselves, and how parts of the body should be organized in relation to other parts. Finally, not only does it say that mind and body cannot be separated in practice, but it shows precisely how they are interconnected.

What is the Alexander Technique?

The core of the Alexander Technique has to do with the *use of the self* – the way we move, perform actions, coordinate ourselves in all our everyday activities. This has implications for our posture, our freedom to breathe, the quality of attention we bring to our tasks and the ease and economy with which we fulfil our purposes. On a physical level, it involves creating the right amount of tension necessary for whatever activity we are undertaking, and a radical redistribution of muscular tone throughout the body. On a mental level it produces a calmer and clearer state of mind: we are less driven by conflicting impulses. Our whole psycho-physical being becomes more harmonious and there is a more balanced use of all our energies.

The primary control

Alexander's main discovery was that all aspects of our functioning – whether to do with our level of skill in activity or in our psychosomatic well-being – are influenced by the way we use ourselves. This 'use' depends on a proper relationship of head to neck to back, which

Alexander called the *primary control*. That is, when the neck is free of undue tension, the head is poised naturally on top of the neck and the spine can lengthen itself. This produces the maximum space and freedom for the lungs to expand, the heart to pump, digestion and elimination to flow and the pelvic organs, including the uterus, to function properly. Joint surfaces are less compacted, there is better tone and lengthening of muscles throughout the body and movement becomes lighter, smoother and easier.

Disturbance of the neck-head-back relationship is so nearly universal that we usually overlook it altogether. It can be particularly noticeable, however, in conditions of stress, whether predominantly mental or physical. The so-called *startle reflex*, which has been observed scientifically, illustrates this clearly. Under threat – and in the laboratory it may be in reaction to the sound of a loud pistol shot – the body immediately goes into survival mode: amongst other things, tension rapidly builds up in the neck muscles, causing the neck to arch and the head to jam back and down towards the shoulders, which hunch. Within half a second, this rise in tension grips the whole body. If the subject is only startled a little, the one group of muscles that may still show a reaction are the neck muscles. Another situation that throws into sharp relief this tendency to shorten the neck and retract the head is bending low or lifting. If you put your hand at the back of the neck you can feel the muscles tightening, especially at the lowest point of bending or when you start to straighten up.

Alexander's story

F Matthias Alexander (1869–1955) had begun to notice a pattern of misuse in himself as a young actor. When he recited, he observed in mirrors that not only did he pull his head back and down towards his shoulders, but he simultaneously raised his chest and hollowed his lower back. This went along with an audible sucking in of air and pressure on his vocal cords.

At a particularly demanding engagement the recurrent hoarseness that had been troubling him became so severe that he could barely speak. His promising acting career seemed in ruins. When he had consulted doctors previously, all they could suggest to him was rest, which only temporarily resolved the problem. They could not answer his query about what he might be doing to create the problem in the first place. He decided, therefore, to find out for himself. At the outset, he thought that it would be quite easy to learn to carry himself differently in order to project his voice properly. It took some time, however, before he began to appreciate what he was really up against in trying to improve matters.

Wanting to change yet remain the same?

Alexander began to see that the faulty pattern of tension which affected him while he was acting was present all the time but in differing degrees: it was just a question of how much stress he happened to be under. By experimentation he had found that the 'attitude' of his head on his neck seemed to affect the relationship of all other body parts, but all his attempts to try to maintain an improved posture when reciting failed; either he made himself generally stiffer or he overcompensated for the retraction of his head and pulled his head forward and down, which put pressure on the front part of his throat. What was going wrong? He hadn't reckoned on the combined forces of *habit* and *unreliable body sense*.

As far as habit is concerned, basic patterns of movement are stored in the back part of the brain, ready to be activated when we initiate activity, just like calling up a computer program. Habitual patterns of muscular misuse go along with an unreliable body sense. As Alexander came to observe finer details of movement in his mirrors, it became disconcertingly clear to him that he was not doing what he thought he was doing – he had *felt*, after some months of practice, that he was successfully preventing this pulling back of his head while reciting, but his mirrors told him otherwise.

His belief had been, up to then, that if only he tried hard enough to change his body use, the problem would be solved. However, he finally realized that all along he had been endeavouring to 'do the right thing' – which meant what *felt* right. Now he could see that what felt right was objectively wrong because it involved the misuse of his whole body and the interference with his voice. And so he was confronted with the question: did he really want to change? If so, that would mean allowing something quite different to happen, which was bound to feel wrong – at first.

Creating change: inhibition and direction
The turning point came when Alexander realized that he only had to think of reciting and his body would begin getting set in the habitual manner of misuse that was so damaging for his voice and performance. So his hoarseness not only was a problem of the way he used his whole body, but was inextricably bound up with how he used his mind in relation to what he was doing: mind and body, in practice, are inseparable.

It was important, then, to prevent the tension pattern from being triggered in the first place. Alexander called this process *inhibition and non-doing*, by which he meant the decision to refuse to respond in the automatic way – leaving his body 'in neutral gear'. He was then free to choose his response. How, exactly, did he do this? He repeatedly practised situations in which he framed the intention of reciting and then he gave himself three options: to recite; to do nothing; or to do something entirely different. So long as he was prepared, most of the time, not to proceed with achieving his end – reciting – then, gradually, he was able to weaken the automatic build-up of tension that began whenever he wanted to recite.

Something else was needed to deal with the underlying tension and to maintain better use of himself when he came to recite: instead of trying to put or keep his head in what he had previously thought was the right position, he would practise *directing* his neck, head and torso into an improved relationship. This was done by projecting 'thought messages' to those parts of the body (and sometimes secondary directions were needed to the arms and legs as well). These directions were, simply: *let my neck be free to let my head go forward and up to let my back lengthen and widen* (and so when we mention the need to *give directions* – as we frequently shall throughout the book – you know what we have in mind). These directions were given without any attempt to 'do' them – to carry them out directly. Their main purpose was to prevent the neck from stiffening, the head from pulling back and down, and the back from shortening and narrowing. With practice, they can be given 'all together and one after the other'.

And so instead of going directly for his end – which always got him into difficulties (he called this *end-gaining*) – through practising inhibition/non-doing and giving directions, by *thinking in activity*, he was able to acquire a powerful and effortless resonance of his voice and he was never again in trouble on the stage.

Use as the 'Cinderella' of health

Alexander also found, to his delight, that his general health and well-being improved considerably and his tendency to various nasal and respiratory disorders disappeared. His interest in the discoveries he had made now began to take precedence over acting, especially as he saw that most people showed similar patterns of misuse. He started teaching other actors about his discoveries and they frequently reported unexpected improvement in their health. Soon he was asked to help people suffering from all sorts of chronic conditions. Doctors were so impressed with the benefits to their patients that they urged him to leave Australia and take his method to London, where it would be assured of the recognition it deserved. This he did in 1904, and began a long career teaching his technique. In his practice, he witnessed many cases where recovery from ill-health went hand-in-hand with the individuals restoring a better use of themselves in their daily activities. Alexander, therefore, felt quite justified in asserting that *use affects functioning*; by 'functioning' he meant all aspects, from the skill with which we perform our everyday acts to our psychosomatic health: the proper working of all body systems, whether those of respiration, blood circulation, digestion, elimination, nerves or the senses or reproduction.

We are constantly reminded today of many of the factors, the 'ugly sisters', that influence health: poor nutrition, pollution, drug abuse, lack of fulfilment. But there is one factor that is often overlooked: the 'Cinderella' of health – what Alexander called the *use of the self*. Just before the Second World War, nineteen doctors wrote to the prestigious *British Medical Journal*, calling for an understanding of Alexander's concept of 'use of the self' to be included in the medical curriculum. Sadly this has not happened, although many individual doctors, over the years, have been aware of the value of the Technique and have referred their patients for lessons. Certain scientists have also had the highest regard for Alexander's work: among them the eminent physiologist Sir Charles Sherrington. The ethologist (researcher of animal behaviour) Nikolaas Tinbergen, who was awarded the Nobel Prize in medicine and physiology in 1973, had this to say about Alexander and his work:

> This story of perceptiveness, of intelligence and of persistence, shown by a man without medical training, is one of the true epics of medical research and practice.[3]

Although Alexander was not an academic, his work raises some fundamental questions at the interfaces of medicine, education and psychology, a challenge which has been little taken up. It is certainly not easy to pigeon-hole Alexander's work; it is easier to say what it is not. Alexander was very much opposed to any form of symptomatic treatment without a thorough understanding of underlying causes. His technique, rather, is about taking responsibility for our health and well-being. This is a life-long enterprise. Let us see now what, in practice, this involves.

Learning the Alexander Technique

Why have lessons?

Some people come for a course of lessons because they want to ensure that they are functioning as well as they can be and to prevent problems arising in the future. Early pregnancy, then, is a starting point for many women. Performing artists – actors, musicians and dancers – find that the Alexander Technique is of considerable help in the preparation and performance of their art. The majority come, though, because they know that things are not as they should be. Sometimes it is just a non-specific sense of 'dis-ease', a feeling of carrying more stress and distress or being less well coordinated than they could be. Perhaps the most common reason that people seek help is because they have health problems that may have become chronic. The Alexander Technique may be the last resort after trying other practitioners, orthodox and otherwise. So what are the kinds of conditions that the Technique may be able to help? They can be categorized as follows:

- 'mechanical' problems: back and neck pain, the range of 'repetitive strain injuries' such as frozen shoulder, tennis elbow, tenosynovitis and so on, arthritis, flat feet, varicose veins, poor posture;
- stress-related, psychosomatic conditions: headaches, respiratory and gastrointestinal problems, hypertension;
- recovery from chronic illnesses, accidents and injuries;
- psychological distress: depression and anxiety states.

This is by no means a complete list, and the particular relevance of the Technique to women's health and pregnancy will be discussed shortly.

Whatever the problem seems to be the general question posed is the same: *how is body use and coordination being impaired?* The answer gradually emerges as your body sense becomes more accurate and you start to notice and let go of layer after layer of tension.

Are there any short-cuts to learning the Technique? The answer is almost certainly no. Useful things can be introduced and demonstrated in a group setting but, to make substantial progress, individual work is required. Alexander said that if you were prepared to do what he did, then you wouldn't need a teacher; he was an exceptional person. It would be very unusual, in fact, for anyone to succeed on their own because the changes needed are so radical and because we have become so dependent on our faulty body sense. It is much easier to develop existing habits than to 'undo' old ones! At the same time, with a relatively small number of lessons, quite remarkable changes can occur if you are motivated.

What happens in lessons?

The teacher will use the tools Alexander discovered – observation, inhibition/non-doing and direction-sending – to help you move with more lightness and freedom. Gradually, you will learn how to create that experience for yourself in progressively more of your daily activities. She will commonly begin with the example of getting up out of a chair, which nearly always demonstrates far too much muscular effort and strain; or she may ask you to demonstrate the kind of movement that seems to be causing trouble. Beginning, perhaps, with you sitting or standing or lying down, she will use her hands to help you release tension in some parts of your body and to restore tone where it is needed. This 're-sculpturing' of the body is then continued in movement, which she initiates for you. Over a course of lessons, she guides you through a repertoire of movement patterns which form the basis of daily activities. The resulting improved balance of muscle tone and quality of movement will usually feel unfamiliar and strange – at first.

From what has been said so far, the role of the pupil may sound rather passive, but it actually requires a good deal of attention and mental application to *allow* yourself to be moved. With repetition, the quality of your coordination will improve – often dramatically – and your own conscious control and thinking-in-activity will increasingly replace your teacher's hands.

How much time needs to be committed to lessons? It is difficult to be precise about the number and frequency of lessons you will need (thirty to forty minutes each) but, as a rough guide, twice a week for the first month and then weekly for a further couple of months or so would constitute a basic course for producing and maintaining worthwhile improvement.

Let's now outline why the time and effort of learning the Alexander Technique can be so valuable for women in their childbearing years.

Pregnancy and Birth

Pregnancy and preparing for birth

During pregnancy, particularly in the later stages, things are changing very fast. There seems to be a need for constant re-adjustment: no sooner do you get used to one phase than you're on to another! The Technique will help you become more in touch with your body, more sensitive to its promptings and more able to adapt. Ways of bending and moving are naturally called into question as you change shape: for instance, putting on your shoes without pressing uncomfortably on your 'bump'.

In the limited time that is available to you as you look forward to the birth, what kind of preparation for it will be necessary? Odent makes the point that the process of labour is instinctual and therefore something for which a woman needs little preparation. If anything, she must *unlearn* what her conscious mind has acquired, so that her 'primitive' brain can take over and orchestrate labour. The Alexander Technique emphasizes the need for us to exercise conscious control so that we can inhibit our acquired, tension-holding ways of dealing with pain and stress, thereby not blocking our involuntary functions – including the process of labour.

Birth

It is gradually being accepted that it is important for women to feel free to move as they wish in labour. But, as we have seen, there is usually a gap between what we want to do and what we can do: we are constrained by patterns of movement that feel right to us, even if they may produce tension, undue effort or strain.

This has implications for the first stage of labour where you need to be – as much as possible – at ease with yourself. Odent says that for this stage of labour to proceed properly, the woman's own hormones need to be freely secreted: endorphins, the body's natural painkillers, and oxytocin, which stimulates uterine contractions. If she is tense and anxious, then her sympathetic nervous system will pump out adrenalin and other stress hormones, preparing her for 'fight or flight' (our primitive survival mechanism). This inhibits the secretion of oxytocin and slows down or halts dilation of the cervix. With a sound knowledge of the Alexander Technique, it is more likely that you will be able to respond to contractions with less tension (which is a resistance to the process of labour) and be active, if that is appropriate. By carrying less overall tension you will be more sensitive to the signals your body is giving you about what is the right thing to do at each moment in labour.

The 'transition' stage of labour may be accompanied by strong feelings of fear or aggression, which is not surprising when you consider the natural 'crisis' of the birth process. The Technique can help you find a better balance between being paralysed by incredibly powerful emotions and feeling you need to let them 'rip'. And, by being more confident about how your body works, you are more likely to *let* the bearing down *do itself* rather than feel panicked into pushing hard by well-meaning (but sometimes misguided) birth attendants.

What's wrong with exercises?

We are bombarded with messages about the alleged benefits of exercises or fitness training, much of it aimed at pregnant women. How are you to discriminate between the kinds of exercise that might be harmful or those that at least have some potential for good? It is interesting to look over books on childbirth education over the last thirty years or so to see how the kinds of physical exercises they recommend have changed. Whatever fitness methods were fashionable at the time – yoga, or aerobics, for example – show a strong influence.

There are forms of exercise that can be beneficial if done slowly, gently and with awareness that do not have to disturb the neck-head-back relationship. Among these are walking, swimming and some forms of dance and movement: for example, Medau and the slow, flowing movements of Yang-style T'ai Chi. When swimming, avoid holding your head out of the water (which creates excessive tension in the neck) and remember that even exercises in water can be overdone.

In his writings, Alexander queried whether 'doing exercises' was as safe and effective as is claimed by their adherents. First, he made the point that if your body sense is faulty – one consequence of which will be poor posture – it will be as unreliable as a guide in your exercises as it has been in your daily activities. Any form of repetitive exercise – especially if performed quickly – carries the danger of grooving patterns of movement that probably need changing.

Alexander raised two further objections to exercises. One is that we usually try to correct specific problems (poor muscle tone, stiffness, lack of stamina) without really knowing sufficiently how our coordination works as a whole; at best we may shift the problem – for example, tension – elsewhere, but we may create new problems. An example is the 'high' that people often experience when doing aerobic work-outs, which can mask damage to joints and soft tissue caused by bouncing into a stretch. But perhaps the most damaging aspect of doing exercises is that we treat body and mind as though they are separate. However we try to 'do' the exercises, we do not sufficiently appreciate that our habitual 'mind-set' in relation to any activity is always going to operate and replay faulty patterns of movement. We shall reinforce the problems we are trying to solve unless we change our whole approach.

Suppleness Without a reliable body sense, pre-existing tension is expressed in all movements and is likely to be exaggerated in the effort to improve suppleness, increasing the risk of strain. Attempting to squat is one example: however desirable it may be for women to be able to squat as part of their range of active birth movements (as well as in daily life, of course), the real question – which is usually not answered clearly enough – is: What is the *means* by which you can recover the capacity to squat *with facility* and *without strain*? We shall try to show you how, in the next chapter, using Alexander's principles.

Toning　　Many exercises disturb the neck-head-back relationship and produce more tension in already tight parts of the body. You should be especially cautious about performing any kind of sit-ups – even the 'gentler' variations such as 'curl-ups' and 'curl-downs' – or double leg raises. They are supposed to restore tummy muscles which have been stretched and slackened by the demands of pregnancy and birth. While they may succeed in doing so to some extent – and it is not easy to get the balance right (they are frequently overdone and cause strain) – it will be at the expense of creating excessive tension in the front of the neck, a pulling down through the whole body and postural distortion.

Women habitually contract their abdominal muscles in order to achieve a flatter tummy. Persistent tightness here is associated with emotional repression (the solar plexus is an important emotional centre) and a loss of body awareness in the whole abdominal and pelvic areas – the opposite, of course, of what is required during birth, never mind at other times! By restoring and maintaining good body use as a whole, the local changes in muscle tone needed after your birth will naturally come about in a coordinated way; the abdominal and pelvic organs will return to their pre-pregnancy positions and the belly to a natural, gently rounded shape.

Breathing and relaxation methods

Alexander's view was that any attempt to exercise direct control over breathing is potentially harmful. Breathing is a largely automatic process which takes place spontaneously when a proper neck-head-back relationship is maintained. It is often disturbed by our reactions to situations. For example, when we are unduly anxious, the startle reflex can be triggered and breathing becomes rapid and shallow. Forced concentration on a task nearly always involves holding your breath.

It is generally inadvisable to impose a breathing pattern on a particular stage of labour. It will be enough to stay as free and released as possible with a longer and wider back and let the 'intelligence' of your body regulate your breathing rhythm.

What about relaxation methods? Alexander pointed out that these tend to produce a condition of 'collapse', where alertness is dulled and muscle tone so reduced that you cannot respond adequately to the demands of living (let alone childbirth).

To sum up, the Alexander Technique does not treat relaxation, posture, fitness and breathing separately; instead, if offers a clear rationale of their underlying connections in the 'use of the self'; and it shows how you can function better through raising your standard of coordination. With some effort on your part to make the Technique your own, it becomes an invaluable resource to draw on during pregnancy and labour and for the rest of your life.

You might like to regard this book as if you were embarking on a journey. Two things before we set out: like any travel book, this one is not a substitute for being there and experiencing the place directly; and your travel guide is, of course, an Alexander teacher who can show you the way through somewhat unfamiliar terrain. Secondly, use the still photographs – especially those in sequence – not because the Technique is about a series of movements as such, but to try to get a sense of the new quality of movement that the Technique can give you.

Note: You will notice that we show little in the way of exaggeratedly 'wrong' postures. Both our models were in advanced pregnancy and we did not want to ask them to put themselves under undue strain. Penelope, who demonstrates most of the movements, was 38 weeks pregnant and we did not ask her to do any movements on her back (in late pregnancy this may be uncomfortable). Annie was 30 weeks pregnant, and so we see her performing those movements.

2

Early Pregnancy

When you are pregnant, adapting well to all the changes – physical as well as emotional – can be a real challenge. At the same time you may become acutely sensitive to your needs: aches and pains, for example, can be a cue prompting you to consider how you use your body in everyday activities. Improvements made now will not only stand you in good stead for the birth, but can affect your well-being for the rest of your life.

The nine months of pregnancy are conventionally divided into three *trimesters*. In the first, you will be adjusting to the idea – and the reality – of being pregnant. Although there are few outward signs, you feel markedly different: the transition to a new hormonal balance may cause morning sickness, breast tenderness, tiredness and general discomfort. During the second trimester you will begin to notice your baby's movements. Most women feel much better at this stage, with more energy and a growing inner strength; you may have a sense that the 'centre' of life is within you. The last trimester, however, may be uncomfortable and exhausting – quite a test of your endurance – as you approach the birth, sometimes with impatience and apprehension, at other times with elation and eager anticipation.

Whatever your experience of pregnancy, the Alexander Technique can help you stay with the process of change, instead of setting your sights too far ahead. Before we discuss what you can do to improve your body use, let's look in more detail at some of the physical changes brought about by pregnancy.

Changes in Your Body During Pregnancy

Growth of the uterus
During pregnancy your uterus grows in size and weight; at full term its total weight – together with the baby, placenta and amniotic fluid – will

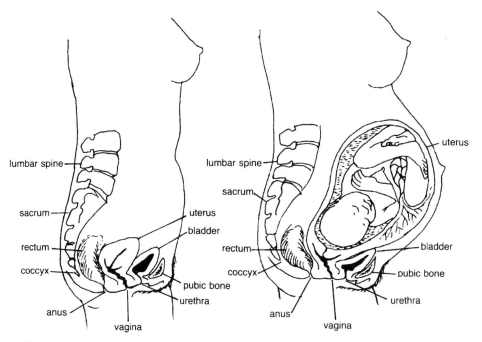

Drawing 1 Uterus before conception.   *Drawing 2* Uterus at full term.

be about 5 or 6 kg (11–13 lb). Your overall weight gain may be two or three times as much. The uterus also changes its orientation in your body. Before conception, its far end (the point furthest from the cervix) points towards the front, with a slight upward tilt. As your baby grows inside you, your uterus expands and rotates backwards so that at the end of pregnancy its far end points almost directly upwards (Drawings 1 and 2).

Using your body well gives you the best chance of allowing this process to take its course unhindered. For example, when standing, you should be poised, without excessive tension in your body (Fig. 1). However, few pregnant women adapt easily to this change. More often than not, the sway-back posture is accentuated: the woman unduly exaggerates her lumbar (lower-back) curve and tilts the top of her pelvis forwards. This makes her look as though she is leaning backwards (although she may feel that she is standing 'straight'). At the same time, her neck is pulled forward out of line with the rest of her spine, and her knee and hip joints tend to lock (see Fig. 2). The excessive tension in her lumbar area and overstretching of her abdominal muscles often cause backache and other symptoms.

Increased flexibility

As your pregnancy progresses, you may notice that you are more supple than usual, due to the softening of the ligaments around your joints. This is caused by the action of hormones, mainly *relaxin*, in preparation for labour and birth: the passage of the baby through the pelvis will be made easier. However, the increased flexibility of your joints also makes them less stable and more vulnerable to injury, and this is exacerbated by misuse. For example, if a sway-back posture is adopted, the joints in the lumbar area of the spine may become too mobile, further exaggerating the spinal curvature. Since extra effort is being made to maintain balance, the ankle, knee and hip joints take more strain. This is why so many pregnant women twist their ankles and also suffer from backache.

Is backache inevitable?

It is widely accepted that backache is a 'normal' part of pregnancy. Various exercises are commonly suggested for alleviating the pain. In most cases, however, backache is caused by long-term misuse of the body; performing any kind of physical exercise without a clear understanding of the primary control is likely to reinforce this habitual misuse, and may make matters even worse.

Some of these exercises are, in our view, particularly undesirable because they inevitably compromise the neck-head-back relationship. It is best to avoid repetitive exercises that require you to roll your head and tilt your neck back and forth in relation to the rest of your spine,

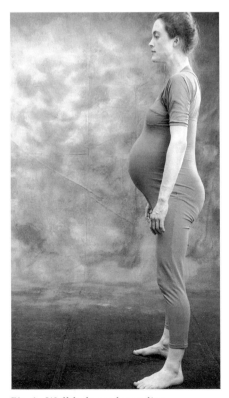

Fig. 1 Well-balanced standing.   *Fig. 2* Unbalanced standing.

interfering with the primary control. The same caveat applies to repetitive exercises that require you to do one or more of the following:

- bending from your waist while locking your leg joints (for a detailed discussion of this, see p. 33).
- hunching or arching your back, which shortens it and compresses your spine;
- twisting your back while bending sideways, which can distort your spine.

Momentarily these exercises increase the blood flow to the lower back and therefore seem to provide some relief from pain, but in the long run they can damage discs and other joints in the back.

It is, however, possible to make movements of the spine without doing yourself harm when you are in 'monkey' (see p. 34), while giving yourself directions and allowing your back to lengthen and widen.

Some pregnant women seek the help of an Alexander teacher after they begin to suffer from backache, and may then gain considerable relief. Prevention, however, is better than cure. Women who have had lessons in the Technique are very much less susceptible to backache when they become pregnant.

> 'Probably the best piece of advice my teacher gave me was to stand with one leg slightly in front of the other, my knees slightly bent. I found I was able to balance my weight easily – and I had no temptation to arch my back.'

Varicose veins

Varicose veins sometimes begin or worsen during pregnancy. This change is usually attributed to two causes. First, the hormone progesterone – which is secreted in greater quantity during pregnancy – relaxes the muscles in the veins and increases their tendency to swell. Second, the growth of the baby increases the pressure on the pelvic veins and slows the return of the blood from the legs to the heart; this causes pressure to build up in the leg veins.

A third cause, which is rarely mentioned, is misuse of the body, particularly persistent locking of the leg joints during ordinary daily activities such as standing, walking or climbing stairs, and sitting in a collapsed manner or with the legs crossed. Wearing high-heeled shoes makes matters even worse: in time, muscles at the back of the leg (which are connected to the Achilles tendon) shorten and the flexibility of the ankle is reduced. Also, the lower back will be considerably more stressed when bending. High heels should not be worn for long periods even when you are not pregnant. During pregnancy, they are best avoided altogether.

If you suffer from raised or varicose veins, you can gain relief by spending some time each day with your legs raised to a higher level than your heart. Lying in the 'semi-supine' position as described on p. 45 ff., support your legs on pillows placed lengthwise under them, from the thighs to the feet. Allow your legs to roll outwards a little, the knees soft and relaxed. Beware of raising your legs too high or keeping them straight: the knees will then tend to lock, pressure at the hip area will be increased, and your blood circulation will be impeded. Some of the movements on p. 56 ff. may also help.

Although your hormones may make you more vulnerable to varicose veins, your improved body use may prevent them from worsening or developing in the first place. The orthopaedic surgeons who wrote *Body Mechanics* noted:

> We have observed frequent relief from varicosities where the only treatment was the correction of the faulty body mechanics.[1]

Other health problems

Many of the other complaints commonly experienced in pregnancy are also related to hormonal changes and the growth of the uterus but are exacerbated by body misuse. These include haemorrhoids (piles), heartburn, varicosities of the vulva, abdominal (bump) pains, breathlessness, cramps, and oedema (fluid retention) in the ankles, legs and hands.

As your body use improves, so will your muscle tone and circulation, and you may find that certain symptoms are alleviated. Some of the movements we shall describe later may also bring relief.

Can misuse affect the baby?

It is well established that poor diet and smoking during pregnancy have long-term effects on the health and well-being of the child.[2] It is possible that body misuse may also have adverse effects. Faulty coordination interferes with the normal relation of the abdominal organs to each other; this may restrict their blood supply and create a less than optimal environment for the development of the baby.

Misuse will not, of course, stop the growth of the baby and uterus – foetal development is highly adaptable and can proceed even in the presence of relatively severe obstacles. Nevertheless, it makes sense to do all you reasonably can to protect the future health of your baby – and improving your own body use may help you both.

Emotional stresses

Pregnancy can bring with it deep emotional changes; life will never be the same again! These psychological aspects of pregnancy affect body use and are in turn affected by it.[3]

Our culture instils in many of us an ambiguous attitude towards our bodies. Women, in particular, often have a negative self-image. If you are not entirely at ease with your body, the changes brought on by pregnancy can increase your ambivalence. As an expectant mother you may receive very mixed and contradictory signals. On the one hand, you are complemented on your radiance and told how special you must be feeling. On the other hand, in a society dominated by images of slimness, many pregnant women find it hard to accept their growing size: they feel ungainly and unattractive.

You may be much more vulnerable than usual: even little upsets may cause you distress. This heightened sensitivity is quite normal (it may even help you prepare for becoming a mother and responding to the needs of your baby). Also, you may, understandably, have fears about childbirth itself.

However, if you let yourself become too wound up, you may set a pattern that will be hard to change. Mental and physical tensions reinforce each other. Adrenalin-like hormones (catecholamines), produced under stress, affect the breathing, the blood circulation, the digestion and all other systems of your body. Learning how to release tension and stay calm will be better for your general health and well-being, and for the development of your baby.

In recent years, excessive technological interference in pregnancy and childbirth has rightly been challenged and the case for natural birth strongly argued. But if we do not know how to make good use of our minds and bodies during pregnancy and labour, it is more likely that technology and drugs will take over. Unfortunately, this is what happens to many women who want a natural birth. To avoid such interference we need to re-educate ourselves, our minds as well as our bodies.

'I decided that my confidence needed a boost and so I enrolled on a course of antenatal classes and also joined a class of Alexander Technique for Pregnant Women . . . these classes made all the difference the second time round, as I was able to really prepare for the birth. I could air my fears about the first birth [which ended in a Caesarean section] and get the risks of a repeat performance into some kind of logical context. I felt my confidence slowly creep back and realized that my body needn't let me down a second time. The Alexander classes gave me such insight into the importance of correct posture and movement, both in labour and in life in general, and I always left feeling energetic and positive. It would be dishonest of me to say that I did not harbour nagging doubts at the back of my mind that my delivery would not go as planned, but I was able to reach the stage of shrugging my shoulders and saying to myself that I had done as much preparation as I felt was possible and now nature must be allowed to take her course.'

Body Use in Everyday Life during Pregnancy

As your pregnancy progresses, the everyday movements which most people take for granted suddenly give pause for thought: getting into a car, lifting a toddler, climbing stairs, sitting at a desk – all become more of a test. Unless you re-think your movements you may find yourself going more out of kilter, or even developing new harmful ways of compensating for your growing size and weight.

> 'Before the birth of my first child, I went to exercise classes for pregnancy. I enjoyed these – meeting other women – as I was new to the area and knew no one with children. Towards the end of my pregnancy, I was a little offended when an old friend commented . . . "You are walking like a duck, like all pregnant women . . ." There had been no mention of how we should *be* outside the classes, except to spend extra time each day practising the exercises.'

The Alexander Technique can help you in this re-evaluation. In the course of your lessons the teacher guides you through basic everyday movements such as standing up, sitting down, lying down, walking, bending and lifting. The repetition of these movements, with improved coordination, sets new patterns of body use. Your sensory awareness gradually heightens and you learn how to carry over the improvements into your daily life.

When you are on your own, however, you may find yourself lapsing into your old habits of misuse. Remind yourself that change takes time and that old habits die hard. The fact that you are now beginning to *notice* tension or collapse implies that they are losing their hold on you. Do not rush to 'correct' whatever is wrong. Notice your position in space and give yourself directions.

We shall now discuss in detail these everyday activities.

Sitting

Alexander pointed out that the slumped posture that many people adopt when seated is a major cause of body malfunction and general ill-health. Most of us spend many of our waking hours sitting, and in pregnancy this can become increasingly uncomfortable.

From an early age, Western women are encouraged to sit with their knees close together or their legs crossed. These sitting positions are regarded as elegant and feminine (although sitting with your legs crossed was considered very unladylike until not so long ago!), but they create unnecessary pressure on the legs and lower back.

When you cross your legs, the weight of your body shifts to one side, causing the other side of the pelvis to rise and twist the lumbar area. At the same time the weight of the top leg constricts the veins in both legs, impairing blood circulation, a contributory cause of varicose veins. After a while, the supporting leg goes numb, giving you a warning signal. Most people react by re-crossing their legs the other way.

The habit of crossing your legs is comparatively easy to break. Whenever you catch yourself doing it, simply say to yourself 'There I go again!' and uncross them. You will soon be able to stop yourself just as you are about to cross your legs. Your new awareness will gradually become second nature.

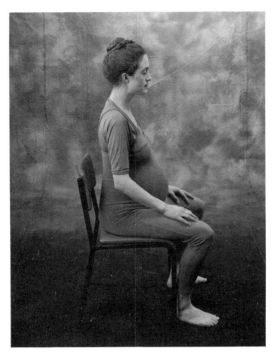

Fig. 3 Sitting at ease.

Sitting in a lesson A considerable part of an Alexander lesson is spent with you sitting on a chair. Sitting is regarded as a *dynamic activity* – a movement or action – not a *static position*. While giving you directions through her hands and encouraging your thinking-in-activity, the teacher will centre your weight over your sitting bones and help you discover a released upright posture, neither collapsed nor too stiff. By gently tilting you backwards and forwards, she will make you aware of your sitting bones and the free movement of your upper body, as a whole, over your hip joints.

She will remind you that while your weight rests on the chair and your feet on the floor you need not tense your legs; you can allow your knees to go forward and slightly out. In time you will find it easier to sit without strain (Fig. 3).

Sitting in everyday life Chairs are not, in general, well designed for sitting. Car seats, for instance, are notoriously bad at providing adequate support for pelvis and back. It is all too easy to slump down and put pressure on your back and abdomen, however much you try to stay 'up'. This is a design fault of most car seats.

The remedy is to use a wedge-shaped piece of foam of the appropriate density (a few centimetres at the thick end) to fill in the trough; to place a small cushion at the base of the seat back if the pelvic support is inade-

Fig. 4   *Fig. 5* Changing position.

quate; and to flatten the contours of the middle of the seat back with more
foam cut to shape (less easy, but worth a try). When all this is in place,
you will find that sitting in a car does not have to be too unpleasant – it's
a golden opportunity to give directions and to get your back nicely
lengthening and widening.

If you are working at a desk, allow your torso to tilt forward slightly, as
a unit, over your hip joints (Fig. 4). The angle at which you sit can be varied continually to prevent fatigue. When using the phone, take the opportunity to change your position (Fig. 5). From time to time get up and
move about. It is best not to stay in your chair for much longer than an
hour.

If you spend most of your working day at a desk, you should adjust
your work station to suit you to prevent unnecessary strain.[4] Ideally, you
should be able to adjust the height and tilt of your seat. The height of
your chair should be roughly a third of your height and if you are using
an ordinary dining chair, make a foam cushion that will tilt you slightly
forwards (about 5 degrees). You should be able to write at a surface that is
at half your height and sloped about 15 degrees. The keyboard should be
at such a height that the forearm is parallel to the floor, the wrist in a
neutral position.

Standing up

Getting up and sitting down are among the most frequent movements in our daily lives: a diligent statistician has calculated that in an average day an average adult moves in and out of a chair about two hundred times!

Let's suppose you are sitting on a chair and you decide to get up. What happens in your body at the start of the movement? What is your immediate impulse? If it is to get out of the chair – to gain the 'end' without attention to the 'means' – then you will take the position shown in Fig. 6. The effort made here is wasteful. The movement begins with arching the lower back and pushing the chest out, causing the muscles of the lower back to contract and pull the body *backwards* and *downwards* when it really needs to go *forwards* and *upwards*. The weight of the baby pulls the tummy down, and this is compensated by retracting the head backwards and downwards in order to move up! This faulty use of the body produces unnecessary pressure on the internal organs as well as on the skeleton.

Standing up in a lesson   Your teacher will remind you to inhibit the desire to achieve an immediate result. She will ask you to give your consent to the movement only after and while you direct yourself. Then the head can lead the movement, the back follows and the whole torso tilts forward slightly, with the hip joints serving as pivots. As your weight

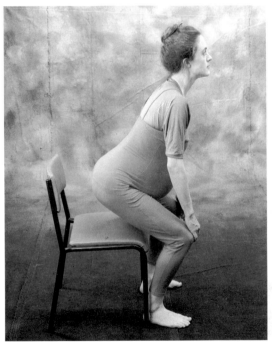

Fig. 6 How *not* to get up from a chair.

transfers from your sitting bones to your legs, your knees are directed forward and slightly out, so that they are aligned with the feet – and you stand up (Fig. 7). While you are getting up, notice that your line of sight moves at a right angle to your torso, so that you do not stare at a fixed point.

Instead of a chair, some teachers occasionally use a big gymnastic ball, about 65 cm (26 in) in diameter. The advantage of the ball is its resilience: it can be a very enjoyable way of becoming more aware of the location of your hip joints as well as allowing your feet to be softer. Bouncing gently will help you explore the movements of your ankle joints (Fig. 8).

Standing up in everyday life   If you are sitting deep in a chair and wish to get up, first shift your bottom to the edge of the chair. During the first months of pregnancy, use your hands, placed at the back of the chair, to help you shift forwards. Make sure that you don't pull your shoulders up. In the last three months, however, when the uterus is much heavier, it is better to 'walk' on your sitting bones, shifting your weight from side to side (with your head leading the movement, your back lengthening and your torso tilting slightly forward over the hip joint), each time advancing the side that does not carry the weight. A few movements will get you to the edge of the chair. Having reached the edge, put one foot forward and, giving yourself directions, allow the getting up to happen of its own accord (Figs. 9–11).

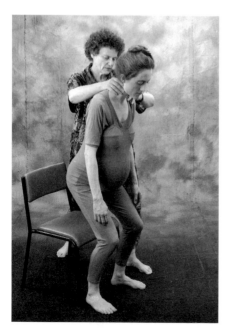 

Fig. 7 The head leads and the body follows. *Fig. 8* Sitting on a ball.

Fig. 9

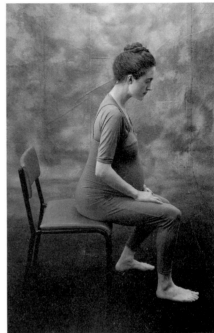

Fig. 10

Fig. 11

Figs. 9–11   Getting up with directions.

Sitting down

If you sit down without giving it a thought, you will probably repeat in reverse the same strained movement as when getting up. In pregnancy, there is a greater fear of falling. Balance may be so uncertain that the pregnant woman compensates by stiffening through her body: while the bottom is searching for the seat, the shoulders are raised, the head is pulled between them, and the lower back is arched.

Sitting down in a lesson Your teacher will give you a sense of security and allay your fear of falling backwards. First she will guide you to find your balance while you are still standing. She will suggest that you stand with your feet shoulder-width apart. She will then ask you to direct your attention not to the chair or the act of sitting, but to the movement itself; while you continue giving yourself directions, she will ask you to let your legs fold underneath you by releasing your ankle joints, bending your knees and letting them go forward and out. If the teacher notices that you lock your hip joints, she will draw your attention to that fraction of a second during which the knees bend and the torso balances itself over the hip joints. The three leg joints – the ankle, knee and hip – need to work together (Fig. 12). Then you will find yourself seated on the chair that was waiting for you – like magic!

Sitting down in everyday life Stand in front of the chair with your calves touching it to give you greater confidence. In advanced pregnancy you may feel more secure if you position one leg in front of the chair and the other slightly back, touching its side.

Standing

By its very nature, standing is an unstable position. Even when you are not pregnant, the front of your body, being heavier, pulls you forward and down; you need to balance yourself constantly on your feet. Most people's habitual way of doing this creates stress: they partially collapse and then tense to hold themselves up. One reason for this is that many of us have a wrong 'map' of our body:[5] for example, the legs may be mistakenly perceived as going up to the hip *bones* rather than to the hip *joints* (which are lower).

During pregnancy, your centre of gravity shifts further forward. Habitual misuse therefore tends to become even worse. Figure 13 demonstrates how harmful use is often accentuated in a pregnant woman. Her head is pulled back and her neck sticks forward. Her chest is collapsed, her pelvis inclines forward, increasing the curvature in her lower back. Her hip, knee and ankle joints are locked, and her weight presses down on the balls of her feet. Some women become so much off balance that they need to grip the floor (or the inside of their shoes) with their toes. All this involves a great waste of muscular effort.

Another common faulty habit in standing is demonstrated in Fig. 14.

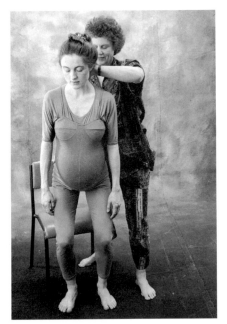

Fig. 12 Being guided to sitting, legs folding underneath the body.

Fig. 13 and 14 How *not* to stand.

Here the weight of the body is supported on one leg, whose joints are locked. The pelvis tilts and sinks into the hip joints, causing severe twisting in the lower back. This habit is very common, and you can easily find yourself slipping into it. Because of the discomfort it causes, however, you will soon want to shift your weight to the other leg. This is similar to what happens when you sit with your legs crossed: the body protests against its misuse. Now is a good time to change the habit altogether.

Standing in a lesson   Your teacher will guide you to stand so that your weight is evenly distributed over the whole of the soles of both feet. She will ask you to widen your base by standing with your feet apart, so that they are roughly under your hip joints. This stance minimizes the effort of balancing (Fig. 15). While giving you directions, she will draw your attention to your feet and your leg joints, and will ask you to release these joints, especially the knees. With improved use, you will be able to adapt more easily to the rapid changes in your body, particularly in the later stages of pregnancy (see Fig. 1).

At first, when you are guided into a new balance you may feel as though you are about to fall forwards. The deceptiveness of this sensation may be easily demonstrated by looking in the mirror.

Standing in everyday life   If you need to stand for a prolonged period, it may be more comfortable if you change your stance from time to time

Fig. 14

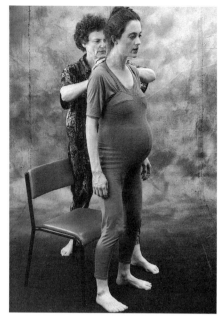

Fig. 15 Being guided to a better balance.

by putting one foot slightly forward. This also aids circulation and may help to prevent varicose veins.

Bending

Bending at the waist with locked knees is both inefficient and harmful, cramping your internal organs, including your uterus and your baby. This cannot be good for you or your baby (Drawing 3). Unfortunately, many classes and books for pregnant women recommend exercises in which the legs are kept straight, and bending is done from the waist rather than from the hip joints.

The spine does not contain hinge joints: the small joints between the vertebrae are not designed for major leverage. For this reason, repeated bending at the waist can damage the vertebrae as well as the cartilage discs between them. This damage is a major cause of pain in the lower back. During pregnancy the risk of harm is even greater, because of the effects of the hormone relaxin. If you don't make a habit of using your legs well, you may find bending increasingly difficult as you put on weight.

The body's major joints of leverage are in the legs: the hips, knees and ankles. When you use the legs as a whole in bending, so that each of the joints has its proper share in the movement, the body is nicely balanced at each link and the distribution of muscular effort is even. The back does not need to bend and there is therefore no pressure on the internal

Drawing 3 A wrong way to bend.   *Drawing 4* The 'monkey'.

organs.[6] (Drawing 4) This is what Alexander called 'a position of mechanical advantage' and has come to be known as the *monkey*.

The monkey   You begin by standing with your feet apart, toes pointing slightly outwards. While encouraging you to give yourself directions, the teacher will guide you to release your knees forward and out, so that they do not pull in but bend above the toes (Fig. 16). Next, with your consent, she will gently incline your torso forward over your hip joints. This is a dynamic tilt, in which the head leads the movement and the back lengthens and widens, while the knees need to bend a bit further. She will remind you not to tense your buttock muscles. Your arms should hang freely and she will make sure that they do not pull the shoulders down and round, but that you continue to widen your back and breathe freely (Fig. 17).

When you have more experience, you will find it easier to make this one continuous movement. The degree to which you bend your knees as well as the angle of inclination of the torso, vary according to what you need to do. For example, you can use the monkey for buckling your shoe (Fig. 18).

The monkey is very useful in daily life and is invaluable during childbirth, when it can form the basis of a whole series of movements; moreover, it is also a preparation for squatting, which will be discussed in detail later.

Fig. 16 and 17 Being guided to monkey.

Fig. 18 Using the monkey to buckle your shoe.

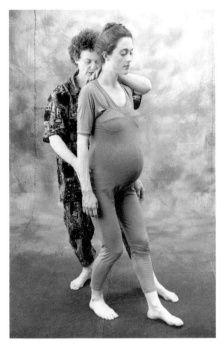

Fig. 19

Fig. 20

Fig. 21

Figs. 19–21   Being guided to lunge.

Lunge This is another bending movement, involving a powerful shift of weight forwards or backwards. It prevents stooping and can be applied in many everyday activities such as pushing and pulling a piece of furniture, a trolley (cart), baby carriage or a pushchair; sweeping; ironing; bending down to an oven; loading and unloading a car; opening and shutting a door.

Your teacher will show you the range of this movement. Once again, you start from a standing position, with your feet roughly hip-width apart. She will direct you to transfer your weight on to (say) the right foot, while your right knee bends slightly. Then she will guide you to turn your whole body to the left through about 30 degrees, with your head leading and your right leg serving as a pivot; at the same time you lift your left leg, bending the left knee slightly, and take a small step in the direction in which you are now facing (Fig. 19).

Next, in a continuous movement, most of your weight shifts forward on to your left leg, while you allow the knee to bend. The teacher will ask you not to clench your toes, letting your weight be distributed evenly on your left sole. Your right foot stays behind, heel flat on the floor, and your arms hang freely (Fig. 20).

She will then guide you back to the initial position and then further back, so that your right knee bends, the leg taking most of the weight of your body (Fig. 21); then again forward and backward several times, ending in the initial standing position. At each stage you are reminded to renew the lengthening of your back.

The movement is then repeated on the other side.

Using your arms

Another common misconception about our 'body map' is that the shoulder is part of the arm. As a result, the shoulder is needlessly lifted when the arm is moved.

We discussed earlier how tension in the shoulders and neck is also produced by the 'startle reflex', which is activated in every one of us many times each day in response to sudden stimuli. The trouble is that we forget to release the tension and so we remain in a 'startled' posture long after the stimulus has vanished. You can observe this while driving, especially when you are in a hurry or tired: notice all the tension that accumulates in your neck and shoulders, and the way you find yourself gripping the wheel. Instead of getting annoyed by a red traffic light, regard it as a friend: it gives you an opportunity to relieve any tension while you are waiting for the lights to change.

During pregnancy, releasing tension in arms and shoulders is particularly important. Some pregnant women experience stiffness or weakness in their arms and hands, often after waking in the morning. This can be caused by an accumulation of fluids (oedema) but may also be a result of the pressure exerted on the arm by the body's weight in an awkward sleeping position.

Fig. 22   A wrong way to raise arms.

Fig. 23   The back lengthening and widening while arms are raised.

When the arms are used well, the shoulders are released sideways, away from each other, the back lengthening and widening in the movement; the arm is lifted away from the back, with the hand leading.

Work on the arms in a lesson can be very enjoyable. Your teacher will 'play' with your arm: she will ask you to give yourself directions while she moves your arm in various ways. You will gradually acquire a new awareness and understanding of the articulation of your arms and learn to gauge more accurately the amount of effort needed for using them. In time you will be able to apply this in your everyday movements. Notice the differences in the pictures: in Fig. 22 the shoulder is unnecessarily lifted together with the arm; this stiffness of the shoulder is compensated by an excessive arching of the lower back, pulling the head backward and down, and locking the leg joints. In Fig. 23 see the improved coordination overall.

Fig. 24 shows another everyday movement of the arm. Notice the lightness and ease with which the arm moves to reach the phone and lift the receiver, and compare this with the tense and effort-wasting movement in Fig. 25. While we are on the phone, see the contrast between Fig. 26 and Fig. 27.

In everyday life we often lean on our arms, supporting part of our

Fig. 24 Reaching with ease.

Fig. 25 Pulling the head back while trying to reach.

Fig. 26 Wrong way of using the phone.

Fig. 27 Right way of using the phone.

weight on the elbows, fingers or knuckles. As your body weight increases, you may find yourself wanting to do this even more frequently than before, creating unnecessary pressure on all the joints of the hands and arms and tension in the shoulders and neck. Instead, use the *whole* of the palm to help support the weight (Fig. 43).

Good use of the arms and hands can help to prevent the 'carpal tunnel' syndrome, a condition whose incidence is higher among pregnant women than in the general population. This syndrome can cause disabling numbness and pain in the hand, wrist and forearm.

Lifting and carrying

Now that we have looked in detail at ways of bending, here are some basic guidelines for lifting. These guidelines are widely recommended to all pregnant women, particularly when you need to bend very low. However, in themselves they are insufficient: the important thing is not only what you do, but how you do it. By giving yourself directions – reminding yourself not to pull your head backward and down as you lift, but to lengthen your back you can avoid misuse and its ill-effects.

- Before you lift an object, make sure that you get close to it, facing it squarely, not sideways, to avoid twisting your spine.
- First go into a lunge, then bend your knees further; let your legs provide a flexible powerful base, so that arms, shoulders and lower back take little strain.
- Pick the object up by placing your hands beneath it in order to provide an efficient leverage.
- Whatever the weight of the object, relax your arms and shoulders as much as you can and lengthen your back as you lift rather than shortening and contracting it.
- Carry the object as closely as possible to your body.
- If the object is heavy or bulky, lift it in several easy stages (Figs. 28–31).

Often the object you want to lift lies not on the floor but on a low piece of furniture. It is very tempting to bend your back rather than your knees, but this will set up cumulative strain. Whenever you need to bend at all (Fig. 32), try to approach the movement with the same care and attention you give to difficult lifting. Good habits will carry over into more demanding movements.

Walking

Walking is rightly considered to be good general exercise for pregnant women. The trouble is that when we go for a walk we take with us our habits of misuse. The woman who stands badly will walk badly. While transferring her weight from one foot to the other, she tends to sink on to the leg that receives the weight and to lock its joints, causing unnecessary pressure and tension. In addition she often swings her shoulders from

Fig. 28

Fig. 29

Fig. 30

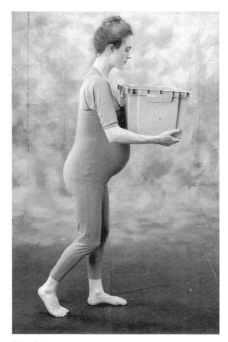

Fig. 31

Lifting a box in several stages.

Fig. 32   Lunging in order to lift.

side to side, causing harmful twisting in the lower spine.

As you gain more understanding of the Alexander Technique, your walking will gradually improve. When the neck muscles are releasing, with the head poised and leading the movement, there is a definite lengthening force acting upwards, countering the downward pull of gravity and giving you a sense of lightness. The torso remains centred; the arms hang freely from the shoulder joints and swing gently with the motion. You can see this in Figs. 33–35. As Penelope transfers her weight on to her right leg, her head leads and her back lengthens. Notice how, when the whole of her weight is balanced on her right foot, her right knee remains slightly flexed. The left foot then 'peels' away from the floor, heel first; and as the head, neck and torso move forward (and up), she lifts her left knee to move her foot forward, ready for the next step. Her arms accompany the movement without the shoulders twisting.

When walking, remember to take your Alexander directions with you! It can be helpful to pause from time to time and ease out of any pulling down that may have occurred, before going on.

Going up and down stairs   A pregnant woman walking upstairs can look a sorry sight. She makes it seem more strenuous than it need be. As she is transferring her weight from one leg to the other she presses down on the banister, pulling her head back and sinking on to the joints of the receiving leg; and then she locks the knee of that leg and jerks it backward as she heaves herself upwards and places the other foot forward.

Of course, going upstairs does require more effort than normal walk-

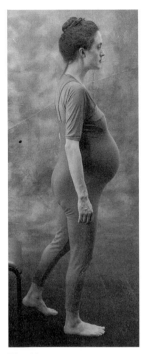

Fig. 33   *Fig. 34*   *Fig. 35*

Walking without tension.

ing, but the general pattern is similar. There is no need to press your weight down on the banister; rather, it is used for stability, allowing the long muscles of the legs to do the work for which they are suited, the head leading the movement (Fig. 36). The whole body is kept in balance.

When going downstairs you will keep your balance more easily and be safer if, instead of facing directly downstairs, you angle yourself at about 45 degrees towards the banister (Fig. 37).

When going upstairs or downstairs the movement should be continuous and flowing rather than jerky, and the head should move more or less in a straight line rather than in a zigzag.

Lying down

Lying down in the 'semi-supine' position with two or three paperback books under your head is so strongly associated with the Alexander Technique that it has become known as the 'Alexander lying down position'. Indeed, a substantial part of a lesson is usually spent on a table or a couch in this way; you will be advised to lie down for about twenty minutes each day in this semi-supine position, which is described in detail below.

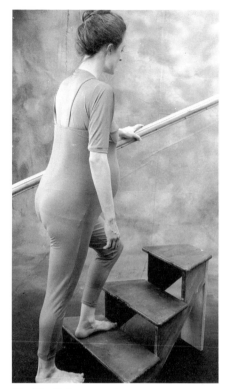

Fig. 36 Going upstairs.

Fig. 37 Going downstairs.

Practical Work in Early Pregnancy

'Relaxation' or releasing tension?

'Relaxation' is the buzz word in all books on pregnancy and childbirth, as well as in antenatal classes. Unfortunately, most people think of relaxation as passively letting go, which is certainly not what is required in labour. Merely giving in to gravity, whether in movement or at rest, does not lead to relaxation but rather to *slumping*, in which, paradoxically, parts of the body become very tense in order to prevent total collapse. Over the years, most of us have acquired poor habits of body use. Therefore, when asked to choose – without expert guidance – a 'comfortable position', people will almost invariably choose a position that initially *feels* comfortable to them, but which is bound to conform to their tension-creating habits. This is where the help of an Alexander teacher is essential to enable you to discover the special dynamic release that avoids both tension and collapse.

As part of a course of lessons, you will need to set aside a period of about half an hour each day for *dynamic relaxation* as well as special practice in applying the Technique to activity and movement. To do this work you do not have to be athletic: anyone can learn to improve their coordination. The most important thing is to practise regularly.

The semi-supine position

An excellent way to learn to release tension is to lie in a *semi-supine* position on the floor, with knees bent and pointing upwards and head resting on a low support (see Fig. 45). It takes the body about twenty minutes in this position to recuperate from normal, everyday stresses. One of the advantages of this position is that it allows the discs between the vertebrae to expand and the big joints of the body to separate, so that there is more space in the joints and less pressure. Also, when you are lying in the semi-supine position, there is less pressure on your internal organs, including the uterus.

In late pregnancy, lying on your back may feel uncomfortable because the weight of the baby and uterus exerts pressure on the large blood vessels in the lumbar area. For late pregnancy you may prefer other positions (see p. 80).

Working on the floor in the way we shall describe can be very beneficial for achieving real rest for body and mind – vital for resolving the physical and mental stresses that accompany pregnancy. It promotes dynamic, deep relaxation.

Your first impression may be that the instructions are somewhat tedious, complicated and difficult to follow. However, after taking lessons and receiving guidance from your teacher, you should find that if you read the instructions carefully you will be able to carry them out without difficulty. To make it easier, you can ask your partner or a friend to read them out to you while you are moving and lying down: it is a good idea to involve your partner or a friend in your preparations for birth. Alternatively, you may tape the instructions and play them back to yourself. Don't rush. If necessary, repeat a phrase or a passage. All your movements should be smooth and continuous. Try to avoid jerkiness and do not hold your breath. Keep reminding yourself to 'think–in–activity'.

Prepare a clear floor surface, preferably carpeted, on which you can lie down, turn and crawl unhindered. Wear loose comfortable clothes such as a track suit and take off your shoes; and make sure you keep warm.

From standing to lying

From standing to kneeling   Stand with your feet a little apart. Be aware of your head balanced on the top of your spine. Look out in front of you and gently turn your head from side to side following your eyes, to help ease any tension around the head and neck. Release your jaw and soften your mouth, gently breathing out.

Be aware of your shoulders; let them release and spread sideways, all the while reminding yourself to free your neck and to let your head go forward and up. Let your arms fall by your sides, down from your shoulders.

Fig. 38 Well-balanced standing.

Be aware of the length of your back from your neck to your tail-bone (coccyx). Be aware of the width of your back between the arms on either side. Allow yourself to expand into the length and width of your torso. Listen to your own breathing, which should occur effortlessly and rhythmically.

Be aware of your legs, from your pelvis to your feet. Soften and unlock your knee-joints. Let your feet rest on the ground, allowing the ground to support you. Your weight should be distributed evenly on the soles of your feet. Direct your knees slightly forward and out, so that each knee is above the ball of the foot.

Now let your attention rise slowly through the whole length of your body, and re-direct (Fig. 38).

To go from standing to kneeling, take a step forward – say with your left foot – and kneel on your right knee; now bring your left knee down and back, so that you are kneeling on both knees (Figs. 39, 40).

Kneeling on all fours   Pause to renew your directions. Letting your hips fold underneath you and, allowing your back to lengthen, lower yourself on to your heels, sending your torso and hips back (Fig. 41).

With your head leading again, tilt yourself forwards to kneel on all fours (notice that the hip joints and knees are the pivots of this movement). Supporting your weight on your hands and knees, make sure that

Fig. 39

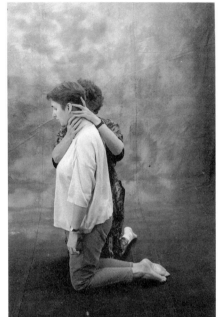

Fig. 40

Fig. 41

Fig. 42

From kneeling to all fours

Fig. 43

Figs 43–44   from sitting on
haunches to lying on the side.

Fig. 44

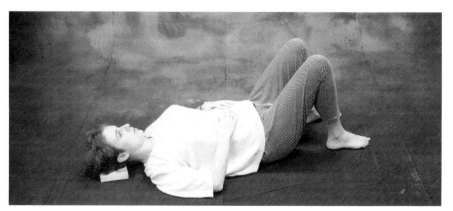

Fig. 45 Lying down in the semi-supine position.

your hands are under your shoulders and your knees under your hip joints. Let the whole surface of your hands touch the floor: if you lean on your fingers or knuckles, you create unnecessary tension. Don't curl your toes, but keep the top of your instep in contact with the floor. Make sure that your neck is free, your face horizontal and parallel to the floor. Don't hollow or arch your back, but allow it to lengthen and widen (Fig. 42).

From kneeling to lying   Interchange 'left' and 'right' throughout in the following instructions if you find it more convenient.

From kneeling, move towards the right until you end up sitting on your right haunch with both legs bent at the knee, the sole of your right foot next to the inside of your left thigh and your left foot behind you. During the movement from kneeling to this sitting position, keep your neck free and allow your head to lead; let your back lengthen and widen while it tilts to the right over your hip joint. You may support yourself on your hands, keeping them flat on the floor and allowing them to take small steps. Pause to re-direct yourself (Fig. 43).

From this position of sitting on your right haunch, move smoothly, with your head leading, into the next position: walk your hands out until you are lying on your right side, your head resting on your extended right arm; both knees are bent, the left slightly more than the right. Pause and renew your directions (Fig. 44).

Now prepare to roll over on to your back. Before doing this, two or three paperback books should be placed on the floor behind your head (you can ask your partner to do this). With your head turning first and leading the movement and your back following and lengthening, turn your whole body on to your back. (You may find it easier to take your left knee in your left hand and bring it closer to your chest as you roll.) Let your feet rest on the floor, supporting your legs. Make sure that your feet are about shoulder-width apart, a foot or so away from your body, and the knees neither sloping out nor held together but pointing straight up to the ceiling (Fig. 45).

The books should be placed underneath your head: they should not be touching your neck. The height of the support varies from person to person, and may even vary at different times for the same person. It depends on many factors, such as length of neck, size of head, curvature of spine and level of stress. If you have too little support, your head will tend to tilt backwards (chin higher than forehead) and it will limit muscular release through the back of the neck and the back. If the pile is too high, your chin will press uncomfortably on your throat. The optimal height is somewhere between these two extremes. The arms are placed with the elbows resting on the floor and the palms of the hands resting gently on the midriff or lower abdomen; the hands should not be clasped.

Lying down   Now you are in what is called the *semi-supine position*. Allow your body to be supported by the floor and your head by the book(s).

Inhibition and directions   This is an excellent position in which to practise giving yourself directions: 'Let my neck be free, in order to let my head release out from between my shoulders, to let my back lengthen and widen and let my knees go up and slightly apart.'

As you allow the directions to take effect, your spine will lengthen and your back widen; you will find that your back will naturally come into greater contact with the floor.

Easing the shoulders and arms   Become aware of your shoulder-blades resting on the floor and let the floor support them. Let the front of your body soften around the shoulders and chest. Let the weight of the arms fall out and away from your shoulders. Allow the floor to support your upper arms and elbows.

Become aware of your upper arms, from your shoulders to your elbows, and let your body open out across the width from your left elbow to your right elbow. Take your awareness back to your head resting on the books. Then move your attention again down to your elbows, observing the space between your head and your elbows.

Become aware of your hands resting on your abdomen. Without moving your fingers at all, bring your attention to each finger, one at a time, and let it be released. Direct your thought back from your hands to your elbows. Be aware of the length of your forearms. Take your thought back to your head, supported on the books.

Easing the back.   Extend your sense of the support of the floor to the whole of your back, all the way from your shoulder-blades and the top of your back to your tail-bone. Be aware of how broad your back is. Enjoy the broad, solid, firm support of the floor under the whole length and breadth of your back.

Let the front of your pelvis soften, and release your lower back. Remind yourself of the whole of your back supported by the floor. Travel in your mind's eye up and across the breadth of your back: up to the shoulders – let them soften once more; then up to the neck – let the neck be free; up to the head – let it rest on the books.

Balancing the legs   Your knees should be directed towards the ceiling, which means a release and lengthening of the thigh muscles from the hip to the knee, and a similar release and lengthening of the calf muscles from the ankle to the knee. In this way your legs are neither 'held' nor floppy, but balanced.

Turn your attention to your legs and feet. Be aware first of your feet on the floor, supporting your legs. Now allow the floor to support your feet. Release the toes. Let them uncurl. Let the balls of your feet be soft. Let the heels rest on the solid ground. Bring your attention to the ankles. Allow them to soften. From your ankles, direct your thought up your shins to the knees. Be aware of your knees pointing to the ceiling and receiving support from your feet on the floor.

Now take your attention from your knees along your thighs to the hip-joints where your legs articulate with the pelvis. Release the tension that has accumulated there. Remember to let your feet support your knees rather than trying to hold your knees away from your hips.

A moment of tranquillity Take your awareness slowly up the length of your body to your head. Check that you have not started to create tension around your neck. Take time to allow your head once again to be supported on the books.

Let your face soften. Release the tension behind your eyes. Let your forehead widen. Unclench your teeth. Let your tongue rest on the bottom of your mouth. Notice your jaw. Are you holding it too tight? Release it. Notice the movement of your abdomen under your hands. Notice also the movement of your ribs. These movements reflect the rhythm of your breathing. Enjoy the gentle pattern of the movement. Make no special effort to expand. Let it happen.

Enjoy the release of congestion and pressure on your inner organs, especially your uterus.

Reflecting on your baby Take a moment to think of your baby growing inside you – this small person that is so close to you, yet whom you hardly know – who is sharing this extraordinary adventure with you.

What image do you have of your baby? Some women like to visualize the baby growing in them; there are books with pictures showing the baby's development in the womb, and looking at these may help you build a stronger sense of your baby.[7]

Taking this time can help you feel closer to your baby. It can also be part of your re-learning to trust in your own body, in its ability to create the best possible environment for the development of your baby and, when the time comes, to give birth.

Getting up When you are ready to get up, don't rush! Move gently and lightly. Now you will reverse the movements that brought you from standing to lying down. Keeping your neck free, move your left knee towards your chest. With your hand leading, slide your right arm along the floor, so that you can roll your head to rest on it. Let your body follow your head and roll onto your side. With your head leading and your neck releasing, you can support yourself on your left hand without pressing down or tensing your shoulder; lift yourself to sitting on your right haunch and then on to all fours.

From all-fours, sit back on your heels. (It is best not to stay sitting on your heels for too long, as it puts undue pressure on the feet. Placing a cushion between your buttocks and heels can make it more comfortable.) Raise yourself on to your knees; with your head leading, bring one foot forwards. Notice that your weight rests on the bent knee. In order to stand up you will need to transfer the weight on to the leg in front. Pause and then let your neck release, to let your head lead you forwards and upwards, away from the bent knee and on to the front leg, allowing your spine to lengthen – and you will find yourself coming up to standing without pulling your head back.

Breathing

Breathing adjusts itself automatically to the physical requirements of the body. Alexander pointed out that there is no need whatsoever for special deep-breathing exercises: we should not interfere with such a spontaneous activity, but create the conditions under which it can occur freely.

Breathing is also affected by our emotional state: anxiety and stress, for example, are accompanied by a whole range of physiological changes and have an immediate effect on breathing.

As your pregnancy progresses, your breathing gradually changes: the rate of respiration may be slightly higher, and each breath is now considerably deeper. As a result, more of the air in your lungs is replaced every minute. This change, which caters for the larger amount of oxygen needed by you and your baby, is triggered by the high level of the hormone progesterone in your body. You may notice that you get more breathless during physical activity.

As an experiment, try deliberately to take a deep breath. You have probably lifted your upper chest, raised your shoulders and hollowed your back; most likely you have pulled your head back and down. (You can also try this experiment on your partner: ask him to take a deep breath and observe the effects on his body.) All of this creates tension and, paradoxically, tends to *reduce* your lung capacity. If, however, you allow your breathing to happen by itself – inhibiting the habit of sucking air forcefully in – your lower torso will expand and your abdominal muscles will release naturally; the upper chest need hardly move. Dr Barlow, who trained with Alexander and was a consultant in physical medicine, says:

> Breathing out, at rest, should last at least twice as long as breathing in. As you finish breathing out, you will feel your stomach muscles contract slightly. In order to get the next breath into your back, you will first have to release this stomach contraction. Many breathing difficulties come from keeping the upper chest and abdominal muscles too tense in front even at rest.[8]

A good time to give some attention to your breathing is when you are lying down in the semi-supine position. However, do not overdo it, because too much concentration on your breathing can disturb its natural rhythm.

The whispered 'ah' This preliminary vocal exercise, devised by Alexander, is often taught in Alexander Technique lessons. It happens to be an excellent preparation for childbirth, as it helps with your breathing and teaches you how to vocalize during labour itself without strain. You can practise it on your own in front of a mirror, or together with your partner, standing or sitting, facing each other.

The important thing, as always, is inhibition and direction. Stop and give directions to your neck-head-back relationship. Now think of a smile; this will help to wet and soften your mouth. Allow your mouth to open. Many people mistakenly believe that the mouth opens by the movement of two jaws. In fact we only have one jaw: the upper 'jaw' is fixed in the skull. When the mouth opens, the rest of the head should not move backwards. If you place your forefingers lightly at the hinges of the jaw – just in front of your ear-holes – it will help you to get a feel of the movement. Do not hold your breath.

Next time, before you let your mouth open, send your jaw slightly forward (so that your lower teeth are in line with your upper teeth rather than behind them). Now allow your mouth to open quite wide. Let your tongue rest on your lower jaw, its tip close to the top of your lower teeth. Keeping your mouth open, breathe in and out a few times through your nose.

Now, breathe out softly through the mouth and allow the breathing in to occur through the nose. You will notice that after you have expelled the air and allowed your breathing muscles to relax, the air streams into your lungs by itself and there is movement in your abdominal wall and lower back, as your ribs move freely. Do not try to push the abdominal muscles: this will only narrow your back. Just notice how they move. As you breathe out, whisper 'aaah'. The sound should be soft and 'round', and your throat should not tighten.

During the first three or four months of pregnancy, do not attempt to do too much. In addition to applying the Alexander Technique in your normal daily activities, the work described so far is quite enough. Avoid jerky movements and do not over-exert yourself.

3

Later Pregnancy

By the start of the second trimester of pregnancy, between the twelfth and the sixteenth week, most women begin to feel better. At the same time, the outward physical changes become more noticeable.

This is a good time to start practising the more active movements described in this chapter. They are designed to help you cope with the changes in your body – especially the distribution of its weight – by encouraging good use and balance. Also, some of these movements begin to prepare you for the actual process of birth.

Don't try to do too much too soon. Remember to inhibit and give directions before and during each movement, paying attention to your neck-head-back relationship. The movements should be flowing and non-mechanical; if you think that you may be making too much effort, or you are aware that your back is shortening during a movement, or that your neck and shoulders have become tense, ask for help from your teacher.

Several groups of movements are described in this chapter. You can vary the sequence of movements, perhaps choosing one or two from each group. Before you begin, read through the instructions and look at the pictures in order to get an overview. Next, imagine yourself doing the movements. Now, as before, ask your partner to read the instructions out slowly to you while you follow them; or you can tape them and then play them back. Gradually, as you master the movements, their inner rhythm will become obvious to you.

Movements from Lying Down

When your teacher works with you while you are lying in the semi-supine position, she will ease your limbs in a certain way. Most of the movements in this group are based on this and are meant to create a similar quality of experience.

During the second trimester, you will probably still be able to lie on

Fig. 46

Fig. 47

Fig. 48

Fig. 49

Lengthening legs on the floor.

your back in the semi-supine position without feeling discomfort. To remind yourself how to get into and out of 'semi-supine', refer to pp. 45–51. If you feel discomfort after lying for a few minutes in the semi-supine position, roll gently over to your side and leave out the present group of movements. Instead, you can do the movements described in 'Lying on your side' on p. 64.

Lengthening your legs

This movement and its variations are particularly useful in relieving tiredness in the legs and feet, helping to prevent cramps, varicose veins and oedema.

(1) Starting from the semi-supine position (see Fig. 45), allow one knee to lower sideways; as a result, only the outer side of your foot (rather than the entire sole) is in contact with the floor (Fig. 46).

(2) In a continuous movement, slide your foot along the floor (Fig. 47) until your leg is extended and resting on the floor (Fig. 48). Re-direct yourself.

(3) Now, sending your heel away from you and lengthening the back of your leg, point your toes towards your body (Fig. 49). Release your leg. Repeat this several times. Check that your neck is not tightening.

(4) Reversing the movements in (2) and (1), return to the semi-supine position.

(5) Observe yourself; re-direct.

Repeat the sequence (1) – (5) several times, alternating legs.

Lengthening your legs – variation   Start with (1) in the basic movement. Then:

(2) In a continuous movement, describe an arc with your knee; allow it first to descend towards the floor and then draw it towards your body (Fig. 50).

(3) Send your heel forwards and upwards, extending the entire leg. (The raised leg now forms an angle of about 45 degrees with the floor.) (Fig. 51.)

(4) Reversing the movement in (3), (2) and (1), return to the semi-supine position.

Repeat this sequence several times, alternating legs.

Lengthening your legs – work with a partner   After some practice you may find that you are able to direct and raise your extended leg higher, so that it forms almost a right angle with the floor. Check again that your knee doesn't lock.

You could ask your partner to help you with this. Get him to stand in

Fig. 50

Fig. 51

Lengthening legs in the air.

front of you, with his feet close to your buttocks. You can then support your extended legs on his body, or he may cradle your heels in his hands and draw them gently upwards (Fig. 52).

Try playing with your legs, 'walking' up and down the front of your partner. Finally, your partner can fold your legs, returning you to the semi-supine position (Figs. 53, 54).

Rolling
This movement and its variations reduce tension in the lower back.

(1) From the semi-supine position, draw both your knees one after the other towards your body: each knee describes a continuous arc as you allow it first to descend sideways towards the floor and then draw it towards the body (Fig. 55).

(2) Hold both your knees with your hands, but without pulling them. Now roll gently from side to side. Remember: the head leads and the spine follows in sequence (Figs. 56, 57).

(3) Roll again to the semi-supine position.

(4) Observe yourself; re-direct.

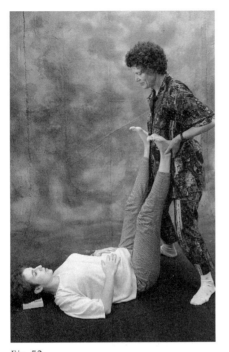

Fig. 52

Fig. 53

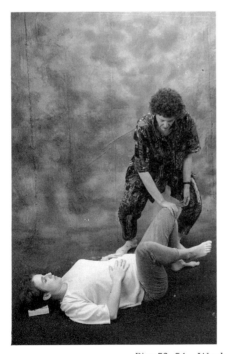

Fig. 54

Figs 52–54   Working with a partner.

Fig. 55

Fig. 56

Fig. 57

Rolling on the floor.

Rolling – first variation   This variation is the same as in the basic move-ment but you should increase the extent of each roll, so that each time you end up momentarily lying on one side, then on the other (Fig. 58). When turning on to your back, let your head lead the movement, with your back following and lengthening. (You may find it easier if you bring your knee closer to your chest as you roll.) Occasionally rest for a few sec-onds on one side (Fig. 59) or in the semi-supine position.

Rolling – second variation   In this variation, when you roll to your right, send your left heel away from your body, extending your leg and allowing the back of the leg to lengthen. Your right knee remains bent (Fig. 60). As you roll on to your back, draw your left knee towards your body (Fig. 61). Now roll over to your left, reversing the roles of the legs (Fig. 62), and so on.

You can combine the theme and the two variations, alternating between them, and vary the rhythm.

Widening the upper back
This movement and its variations help to ease tensions in your arms, shoulders and upper back.

Fig. 58

Fig. 59   Resting on one side.

Fig. 60

Fig. 61

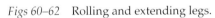

Figs 60–62   Rolling and extending legs.

Fig. 62

Fig. 63

Fig. 64

Widening the back.

Start from the semi-supine position, with your hands resting on your abdomen. Now, keeping your upper arm on the floor, lift one hand in a continuous movement and place it palm up on the floor. Then do the same with your other hand. Your arms end up resting on the floor in the shape of a somewhat flattened W (Fig. 63).

Reverse the movement, returning to the semi-supine position. Observe yourself; re-direct.

Widening the upper back – variations

(a) Synchronize the movement so that, as one hand is moving away, the other moves back on to your abdomen.

(b) Change the angle between your upper arms and your trunk, so that instead of ending up as a W your arms end up resting on the floor in the shape of a very flat V. Remember to release your shoulders (Fig. 64).

Fig. 65

Fig. 66

Fig. 67

Balancing the arms.

(c) Slide your hands and upper arms until both arms are extended side-ways at shoulder height, your palms facing up. Widen across your back, allowing your hands to extend still further. With your upper arms still resting on the floor, lift both your hands and lower arms until your fin-gers point to the ceiling. Lower them gently and move them back on to your abdomen.

(d) Let your arms rest on the floor in a flat U shape. Now lift one arm away from the floor, with the hand leading, until your fingers point to the

Fig. 68

Fig. 69

Fig. 70

Fig. 71

Fig. 72

Lying on one side, lengthening the legs.

ceiling. The whole extended arm is balanced on the shoulder. Do not lift your shoulder blade away from the floor (Fig. 65). Now do the same with the other arm (Fig. 66). Bend your arms and, in a continuous movement, bring your hands back to your abdomen (Fig. 67).

You can improvise your own variations. From time to time stop and re-direct yourself. Make sure that you do not narrow or shorten your back.

Lying on your side

In late pregnancy, if you find the semi-supine position uncomfortable, you can ease your arms and legs while lying on your side. Most of the movements described so far can be easily adapted to this position (see, for example, Figs. 68–72).

Movements from Kneeling on All Fours

Many women find being on all fours a bit strange at first: it is not a usual position for adults, but it is an excellent preparation for childbirth. If you get used to it now, you will probably discover that it is one of the most comfortable positions during labour. In addition, as the baby inside you grows heavier, you will find that kneeling on all fours is a very pleasant way of taking the weight off your lower spine. And, of course, as a mother you will probably spend a considerable part of your time on the floor with your child.

We shall now describe various movements whose starting point is the kneeling position. You may notice that some of them are based on ideas similar to those in the first group (lying down). However, the work of the whole body is quite different, because you will now be orientated differently relative to the force of gravity.

Basic movement from kneeling

Get into the kneeling position as described on p. 45 ff. (Figs. 73–76). Now rock your torso gently back and forth, gradually increasing the range of the movement. At the extreme forward point, your shoulders should be just in front of your hands (Fig. 77); at the extreme backward point, your buttocks should be almost touching your heels (Fig. 78). When your torso rocks backwards, let your arms be free, as they do not need to bear your weight. To end the movement, sit on your heels, pause and re-direct. Remember not to stay sitting on your heels for too long, as it puts undue pressure on your feet. Placing a cushion between your buttocks and heels can make it more comfortable.

Variations

These variations are a preparation for crawling.

(a) As you rock forward, lift one arm lightly up to shoulder height (Figs. 79, 80). Then bring it down. Alternate arms.

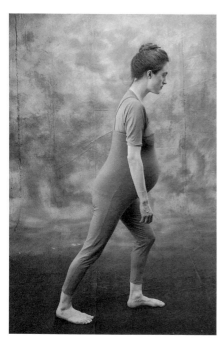

Fig. 73

Fig. 74

Fig. 75

Fig. 76

From standing to kneeling on all fours.

Fig. 77

Fig. 78 Moving torso forwards and backwards.

(b) Turn one hand so that its back lies on the floor. Draw with it a large figure '8' on the floor, allowing your torso to follow the movement of the hand.

(c) Rocking your body slightly on both hands and one knee, send the heel of your other foot backwards. As you rock, allow your elbows to flex (Fig. 81). Release the foot and bring the knee back to the floor.

Crawling

In her book *Sensitive Midwifery*, Caroline Flint recommends crawling from the thirty-sixth week onwards as a means of encouraging the baby to rotate into an anterior position. She notes, however, that many women ignore this advice because 'crawling is very boring'. We think it can be made much more enjoyable by thinking about what you are doing and by tuning into the rhythm of the movement.

Our experience suggests that crawling – particularly in the manner to be described – can be beneficial to *all* pregnant women, irrespective of the position of the baby, because it is a good physical and mental preparation for the process of childbirth.

Fig. 79

Fig. 80

Lifting the arm while on all fours.

Fig. 81

Release one leg.

The best way to learn this procedure is under the guidance of an Alexander teacher. While performing the movements it is very important to maintain a proper relationship between your neck, head and back, as well as the appropriate level of muscular tone.

(1) Start from the kneeling position.

(2) With your head leading, take one small step forward on diagonally opposite limbs, for example on your right hand and left knee, and prepare to crawl. At this point your weight should be evenly distributed on all fours.

Fig. 82

Fig. 83

Fig. 84

Crawling.

(3) Now begin to crawl (Fig. 82): allow the head to lead and move on diagonally opposite limbs. You will notice that when you start each step (leading with your head) your body's weight shifts to the limbs that were in front and are now stationary. After each step, your weight should again be evenly distributed between all fours. Don't rush. Pause. Breathe out gently through an open, soft and wet mouth. Don't gasp, but allow the intake of air to happen gently and effortlessly; your abdominal wall and lower back will expand of their own accord.

(4) As you crawl slowly, don't lift your knee off the floor as it begins to move forward but let it stay in light contact with the floor; your leg will be dragged gently along the floor, pulled forward by the rest of your body, until it is approximately under the hip joint. Then draw it further forward to complete the step. Now your weight should again be distributed evenly between all fours (Figs. 83, 84).

(5) As you get into a rhythm, the crawling should become smooth and continuous. (It may help you to imagine that you are being pulled forward gently by the hair on the top of your head.) The undulating movement shifts your weight from one pair of diagonally opposite limbs to the other.

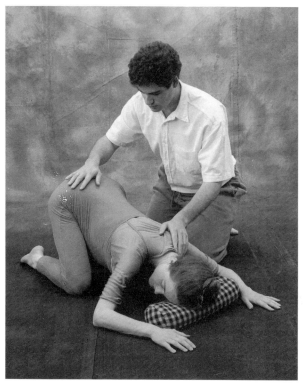

Fig. 85 The knee-chest position.

(6) As you continue to crawl, try varying the rhythm. From time to time pause, think about what you are doing (it is not a mechanical movement!), pay attention to your breathing and let your neck be free.

> 'I had "bumpache" – cramps in the muscles holding the bump – that at times got so severe I could hardly walk any distance. At about six months I came . . . for a session on the application of the Technique to natural birth, during which we did crawling. . . I practised crawling religiously for ten minutes a day, which not only made me feel great but completely controlled the bump pains, so that I was more mobile in the third trimester.'

The breech baby

It is not known what causes most babies to settle in the head-down position after months of floating and turning in the womb: it seems to be a programmed reflex action on the part of the foetus. Although at thirty weeks about one-fifth of all babies are still in breech position, most of them turn spontaneously before birth. Why do some babies (about four per cent) stay in the breech position until the very end? In most cases there is no obvious reason.

If at the thirty-sixth week of pregnancy your baby is breech, there is no cause for alarm: it is quite probable that it will turn spontaneously before birth. There are also some simple steps you can take that may encourage it to do so.

These movements combine dynamically the knee-chest position with crawling.[1] Having taught this technique over several years at special Alexander classes for pregnant women, our experience suggests that it may be effective in encouraging a breech baby to turn. Of course, in the absence of a scientific trial it cannot be ruled out that the cases where it seems to have worked were just a series of lucky turns. Proper research will be required in order to reach firm conclusions.

(1) Crawl as described above.

(2) After you have crawled for about ten minutes, bring yourself from kneeling on all fours to the knee-chest position: lean forward from your hip joints and lower your head down to the floor; spread your knees slightly further apart; allow your elbows to bend until one cheek and both forearms rest on the floor or on a cushion, your hands flat next to your head, allowing your back to widen (Fig. 85). (You can also place cushions under your knees.)

(3) Rest in the knee-chest position for a few more minutes; you will occasionally need to turn your head from side to side. Talk to your baby: 'Turn, baby, turn!'. Then get up again on all fours and carefully rise up to standing. Take care not to lock your knees.

How might these movements encourage the baby to turn? Perhaps the undulation of the pelvis during the crawling and the slope of the torso in the knee-chest position – while the back lengthens and widens – helps to dislodge the baby's bottom from the position in which it is stuck. Then the baby may be freer to perform its pre-programmed turning reflex.

Most of the women who have used this technique report that the turning occurred not while they were actually going through the movements but later, when they were relaxed, for example when taking a bath. Don't expect your baby to turn after the first time you try the movements. Don't give up. The majority of breech babies will turn eventually. However, we must accept that a few will not.

> 'Having had a completely normal and relatively easy birth with my first child, it came as something of a shock to discover at 36 weeks that my second baby was firmly stuck in breech position and that the hospital's policy in such cases was to recommend an elective Caesarean. While the consultant was keen to stress the advantages of this (absolute safety for the baby and less "discomfort" for me), he was also willing to support me if I wanted to try for a spontaneous vaginal delivery. However, the baby would be closely monitored throughout labour and signs of foetal distress would mean an emergency Caesarean under general anaesthetic – he rated my chances of achieving a "normal" delivery at no more than 50 per cent.

'I went away to consider my options, slightly surprised that the hospital's collective obstetric wisdom could not suggest any strategies for trying to persuade my baby to turn. I consulted every book I could find on the subject, all of which suggested that breech babies could and did turn right up until the onset of labour. But hospital doctors, midwives and my GP all agreed that my baby was firmly stuck and, whether delivered normally or by Caesarean, would remain a breech.

'Even though the professionals thought it was hopeless, I knew it would make me feel better if I had at least tried to get the baby to turn. So I spent several sessions a day lying on the floor with my pelvis raised on cushions. After a week or so without progress I consulted Ilana, whose National Childbirth Trust antenatal classes I had attended during my first pregnancy. She immediately suggested that crawling might help and arranged an appointment to show me how to do it. Learning to crawl proved more difficult than I expected, but once I was crawling to Ilana's satisfaction I found it a curiously relaxing activity and crawled around the living room several times a day.

'By this time I had little hope of anything changing but, two days later, as I lay in the bath before my thirty-eighth week hospital appointment, my stomach heaved with astonishing vigour as the baby conducted what was evidently a major manoeuvre. I didn't dare to believe that it had turned a full somersault, but to my delight and the total amazement of the consultant and all in attendance, an ultrasound scan later that morning revealed the baby settled in the normal position for birth.'

Back-to-back with a Partner

Sitting back-to-back with a partner in the so-called tailor position, lengthen and widen your backs against each other and be aware of each other's breathing. Now hold hands and lift your arms to shoulder height (Fig. 86). First one partner supports the other's arms; then you alternate. Remember not to raise your shoulders unnecessarily.

Movements from Monkey and Lunge

The movements in this group – a small selection out of a very large reper-toire – are all based on the monkey (p. 34) and lunge (p. 37). The monkey and lunge are, of course, the basis for a great variety of everyday move-ments. As we shall see in the next chapter, they are especially useful during labour.

Walking backwards

This is not a movement you expect to perform in your daily life. Its role here is to introduce a new concept – moving with directions through space – which may be more easily acquired through unfamiliar movements.

From a lunge, transfer your weight to your back foot (say the left one). As your front leg 'empties', flex your ankle and notice how your body

Fig. 86 Back-to-back with a partner.

turns a little to the left in line with your back foot. Lengthening your spine, straighten your left leg (without locking the knee) as you lean slightly forwards and raise your right knee; let your relaxed foot skate lightly over the floor until it is within a few inches of your left foot. Next, step back by placing your toes (the foot angled at 30 to 45 degrees to the direction you are facing) a comfortable distance behind and to the right of your left foot. Finally, transfer your weight to this leg. Your left foot will naturally turn on the heel to face forward as this leg 'empties'. Pause and re-direct. Now you are ready to repeat on the opposite side.

Walking sideways
This is similar to the previous movement, but the starting point is the monkey (Figs. 87–89).

Balancing on one leg
Starting from the monkey position, transfer your weight to one side, say to the right. With your head leading, allowing your back to follow, lengthen your right leg and lift your left knee to hip level (Fig. 90). Return to the starting position and alternate the legs.

Many variations of this movement are possible. For example, while lifting your knee you can also lift your arms. You can also build up sequences combining the movements of walking backwards, walking sideways and balancing on one leg.

Fig. 87

Fig. 88

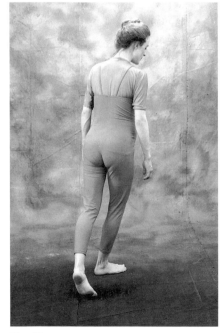

Fig. 89
Figs. 87–89 Walking sideways.

Fig. 90 Balancing on one leg.

Fig. 91

Fig. 92

Fig. 93

Fig. 94

Squatting and rocking with aid of a door.

Fig. 95

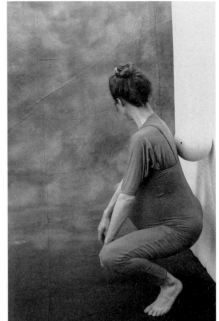

Fig. 96

ig. 97

Figs. 95–97 Squatting with aid of a ball.

Squatting

Squatting is a very advantageous position in labour, particularly during the second stage. Indeed, in many traditional societies women normally squat during birth. Squatting for them is not an unaccustomed position used only for labour, but a normal sitting position for many domestic tasks. Most Western women, however, find squatting very difficult at first. For this reason it is best to learn and practise it during pregnancy. However, an over-eager approach should be avoided, as this will not result in a relaxed squat and will defeat the very purpose of the exercise. It may also damage your knee and ankle joints.

A squat is really a very deep form of monkey. However, to get down to it from an ordinary monkey requires great flexibility in the leg joints, so don't rush it. We shall begin by describing a few easier ways of getting to a squat, using aids.

Using a door

This movement enables you to tilt your torso further back in relation to your knees than would otherwise be possible. It allows your leg muscles to strengthen and your joints to release while being supported.

Stand with your feet wide apart in front of a half-open door. Hold on to both door knobs and lean backwards while you bend your knees, reaching a deep squat. Remembering to keep your neck free, allow your back to lengthen and avoid pulling yourself towards the door. Allow your hips to release backwards as you let your knees bend forward and slightly apart. Keep your arms straight but not stiff. Pause and re-direct. Now swing the door gently, rhythmically rocking your body from side to side. As you shift your weight on to one foot, its heel may rise from the floor (Figs. 91–94). Gently does it!

Using a ball

Assume the monkey position, with your back to the wall. Place a ball (about the size of a football or slightly smaller) between your lower back and the wall (Fig. 95). Roll the ball against the wall with your back. First simply roll it up and down the wall, then from side to side, transferring your body-weight from one foot to the other. Finally, combine the two movements simultaneously, so that the ball describes a circle on the wall (this sounds more complicated than it really is – see Figs. 96, 97). Throughout, send your knees outwards so that they are aligned over your feet and do not fall inwards. Vary the rhythm of the movement. From time to time pause and re-direct yourself.

From kneeling to squatting

This is another relatively easy way of learning to squat. Kneel as described on p. 45 ff. 'Walk' your hands towards your knees (Fig. 98). Next, giving yourself directions, transfer some of your weight on to your

Fig. 98

Fig. 99

Fig. 100

From kneeling to squatting.

Fig. 101 Squatting (profile).

Fig. 102   *Fig. 103*

From squatting to standing.

Fig. 104 Squatting.

Fig. 105 Resting while lying on one side

hands and curl your toes (Fig. 99). Now move your whole torso up and back, ending up with your weight supported on your feet, squatting (Figs. 100, 101). When you want to get up, do so like a child: lift your bottom a little above the floor and then, with your head leading, get up through the monkey position to standing (Figs. 102, 103).

From monkey to squatting

As a result of Alexander work, your legs and back will become stronger and your balance will improve, so that eventually you will be able to squat directly from the monkey position. You will also be able to stay squatting for longer (Fig. 104).

Resting

You hardly need to be told how important it is to rest during pregnancy. Make good use of your rest time, even if you have only an odd five or ten minutes. Also, set aside a longer period for rest after a session of more active movements.

Since in late pregnancy the ordinary semi-supine position may be uncomfortable and should not be maintained for long, we shall suggest some other positions for relaxation and rest. *The first two are also comfortable during sleep.*

Lying on your side

Follow the description of getting to the semi-supine position up to the point where you are lying on your side. Now ask your partner to place cushions under your head and between your knees (Fig. 105). The cushion under your head should support your neck as well, to allow your head to be aligned with your spine.

Resting in the child position

As before, get to the point where you are lying on your side. Slide your arm from under your head so that it is behind your body; at the same

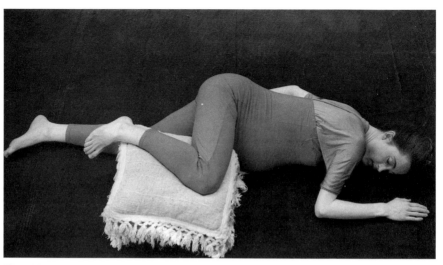

Fig. 106   Resting in the child position.

time roll slightly to the front and ask your partner to place a large cushion under your knee (Fig. 106). There is no need for a cushion under your head: it can rest on the carpet.

Although you may change from side to side, lying on your left side is perhaps preferable because it does not cause pressure on the liver.

Using a gymnastic ball

(a) Kneel on both knees in front of a gymnastic ball about 65 cm (26 ins) in diameter. Rest your torso on the ball (Fig. 107 and also see Fig. 113).

(b) Take up the semi-supine position and ask your partner to place the gymnastic ball under your calves (Fig. 108). Instead of the ball you can use a chair (Fig. 109). Since the ball or chair supports a considerable part of your weight, this position can be quite comfortable even in late pregnancy.

Whispered and Vocalized 'Ah'

Continue to practise your whispered 'ah' (see p. 52), but now add vocalization. First vocalize softly: 'aaah'. Listen to your voice; it should be soft and smooth, not forced. Don't try to go on as long as possible, only as long as comfortable; otherwise you will tend to pull your chest down. As you let the air in through your nose, let your mouth close lightly.

Normally in lessons the student does not go beyond whispering the 'ah'. But in labour you will probably feel the need to vocalize quite loudly, or even shout, so it is a good idea to practise the vocalized 'ah' now. Get used to hearing yourself moaning and groaning (as in passionate love-making!) rather than shrieking.

Fig. 107 Resting on a gym ball.

Fig. 108 Resting with legs supported on a ball.

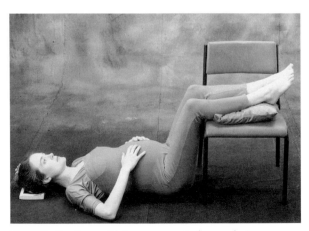

Fig. 109 Resting with legs supported on a chair.

Gradually increase the volume of your vocalization. Remember to re-direct yourself. Ask your partner to listen to you: he should also get used to your vocalization, so that it will not alarm him when you are in labour.

Pelvic Floor Exercises and Massage

The purpose of pelvic floor exercises is to strengthen and, more importantly, to increase the elasticity of the sphincter muscles in that area. Massage of the perineum (the area between the vagina and the anus) has a similar purpose. It also stimulates the blood circulation to these muscles. This enables them to stretch more easily during birth – thereby helping to prevent tears and perhaps avoid the need for episiotomy – and to recover quickly afterwards.[2] Many women say that they have found this particularly useful and believe that it prevented tears during the birth. Another benefit of the exercises and massage is that they heighten your awareness of the action of these muscles, which is so important both in love-making and in labour.

Exercising your pelvic floor
This exercise consists of gently tightening and releasing the muscles of the pelvic floor, mainly those around the vagina. Being able to release these muscles consciously will be very useful during the second stage of labour. It may take you a while to recognize the right muscles; at first you may tend to tighten your abdomen and buttocks at the same time. But as your awareness increases, you will gradually be able to control your vaginal muscles separately.

You can combine this exercise with most of the movements that we have described. For example, you can do it while sitting, standing in the 'monkey' position, or lying. Give yourself directions to avoid pulling yourself down: as you tighten your pelvic floor, let your head go forward and up.

You may also want to synchronize pelvic floor exercises with your natural breathing rhythm: as you breathe out softly, contract the muscles; as you breathe in, release them. Repeat several times. This is a good way of toning these muscles.

Now try another way: while in the 'monkey' position, practise the whispered 'ah'. Each time you whisper 'ah', release your pelvic floor. This is a preparation for what you will have to do during the second stage of labour.

Once again, the important thing is not *what* we do, but *how* we do it. A very common error is to tighten the pelvic floor too suddenly, in a jerky movement, and then release it quickly. This activates the light-coloured muscle fibres, those responsible for *strength*, whereas the red fibres, those responsible for *elasticity*, are underused. If you work your pelvic floor muscles *gently, gradually and rhythmically* – while giving yourself directions – you will find that they will respond better and gain more elasticity.

Massage of the perineum

From about the thirty-fourth week of pregnancy, massage your perineum and the whole of the vaginal area, using vegetable oil derived from olive, almond, wheat-germ or cocoa. You may do it yourself, or get your partner to help you.[3] This sounds pleasant and erotic, but not everyone finds it so; and it can play havoc with your sheets!

Preparing for Labour

During the third trimester you will want to prepare directly for labour. Now is a good time to start practising the movements that are described in the next chapter, so that when the time comes you are thoroughly familiar with them.

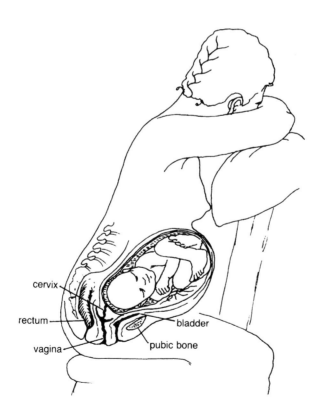

cervix

rectum

vagina

bladder

pubic bone

Drawing 5 Onset of labour – sitting facing the back of a chair.

'As a result of our session I practised on all fours thinking through a contraction, swaying back and forward, rotating the hips . . . This helped keep me comfortable in the last few weeks.'

'When I became pregnant again I had already been having Alexander lessons. This time I didn't do stretching exercises to prepare me for the birth but had a few "top-up" lessons. After the first three months I felt great and was delighted to be able to go on some good long walks in the Dales when I was about six months pregnant. I continued to feel well, and went swimming until the day before the birth.'

4

Giving Birth

No two labours – even for the same woman – are exactly alike: each one is a unique experience. The duration of labour varies considerably from birth to birth, but the essential process is invariably the same – first the cervix thins out and opens (dilates), then the baby is propelled through the birth canal and emerges into the world. Shortly after that, the placenta (afterbirth) is expelled, bringing the birth to an end.

You cannot tell how your labour will begin: most labours start unannounced, with contractions, but sometimes the waters break first (spontaneous rupture of the membrane); for some women labour begins with a 'show', when the mucous plug that seals the cervix comes away, often with some streaks of blood; or it may start in other ways. However labour begins for you, your own active role begins with the onset of contractions; from this point on, maintaining good body use becomes all-important.

The First Stage

The first stage of labour lasts until the cervix reaches full dilation (about 10 cm). This can take quite a long time, usually considerably longer than the second stage – the birth itself – but there are no hard-and-fast rules.

The contractions are triggered by the hormones *oxytocin*, secreted by the pituitary gland at the base of the mother's brain, and *prostaglandins*, secreted by the lining of the uterus. The first few contractions may start gently, or they may take you by surprise and be rather disconcerting; some women feel overwhelmed. But soon you will be able to recognize the signals that a new contraction is about to begin. *This is important because it enables you to prepare to meet it, by giving yourself directions and releasing any build-up of tension.*

During this stage of labour several synchronized processes take place. The uterus contracts rhythmically and retracts: after each contraction, it does not return to its former size but remains slightly smaller. While contracting, it tilts forwards and downwards. At the same time the walls of the cervix become thinner, and it is pulled up and dilates. The baby turns and adjusts itself to the contours of the pelvis as it moves deeper into the pelvic inlet; its soft skull bones are moulded to fit the available space.

The bag of waters (amniotic sac) surrounding the baby may still be intact at the end of the first stage (see Drawing 9). It plays a useful role as a shock absorber and barrier to infection – as it has done throughout the pregnancy. It also has hydrostatic functions: it creates an even distribution of pressure around the baby and balances the natural rise in the baby's blood pressure caused by the contractions of the uterus squeezing the cord. Left to itself the bag of waters breaks either very early on or towards the end of the first stage. There is evidence that rupturing it artificially is quite unnecessary and may adversely affect the course of labour.[1]

Although the process of labour is largely autonomous – controlled by hormones and the involuntary nervous system – it is greatly affected by your conscious activity as well as by your emotions. For example, stress and anxiety may temporarily arrest the progress of labour. Many women report that their contractions stopped on arrival at hospital in early labour. In home births, contractions sometimes slow down with the arrival of the midwife.

> 'The midwife arrived; she had a student midwife with her . . .We were thrilled when she told us I was 7 cm! She phoned for midwife no. 2 . . . who arrived later. She also had a student with her . . . While they organized themselves Clive helped me to do the rocking movements we learnt at the antenatal class. These helped to ease the pain. Though we now had four strangers in the bedroom, I did not feel bothered but Clive says that my contractions did slow down when the second lot arrived.'

Opposite: These drawings show four phases in the first stage of labour. In the first of these, labour is about to begin; the fourth shows the end of the first stage of labour; the other two show intermediate points. To get a clearer idea of how this fascinating process progresses, notice the following three changes.

First, look at the cervix. At the beginning of labour, before it has started to dilate, its walls are still thick. At full dilation the cervix seems to have disappeared.

Second, in the course of labour the uterus contracts and retracts: the muscle fibres of its upper part shorten and its wall thickens. The top of the uterus moves down, exerting a downward pressure on the baby.

Third, the baby itself moves in a remarkable and complex way. At the beginning of labour the baby lies asymmetrically – it is facing towards the mother's left or right side. But as it descends it begins to rotate gradually towards her back. At the same time it flexes its head, bringing its chin to rest on its chest. The crown of the head (where the circumference of the skull is smallest) is in the birth canal. Also, the baby's head changes its shape as it moulds itself into the mother's pelvis. You can get a clearer idea of the baby's journey by drawing an imaginary line between the top of the mother's pelvis and the bottom end of her pubic bone.

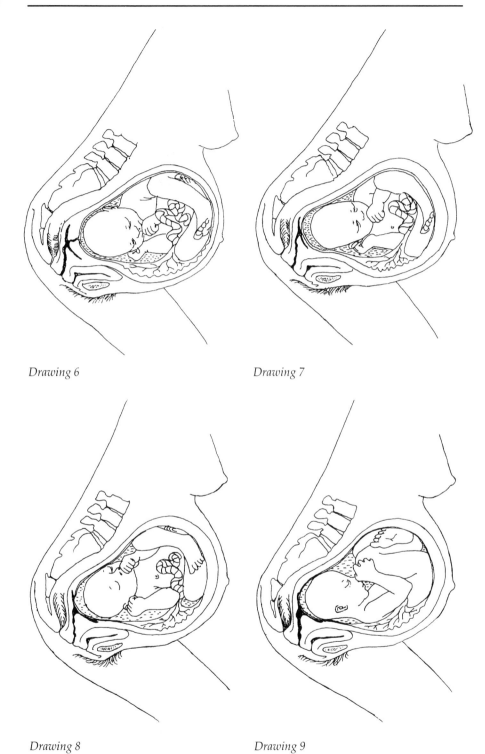

Drawing 6

Drawing 7

Drawing 8

Drawing 9

'I had a show and decided to phone the hospital, as the contractions were now every five minutes, lasting half a minute each. I was told to come in . . . Once installed in the labour ward, I was monitored and my observations taken. I was only 1 cm dilated and the contractions were tailing off . . . My mother and I walked around the hospital and soon enough the contractions started up again with increasing frequency and intensity. Each time one came I held on to her and cried about how painful it was – this was a really useful thing to do.'

Letting gravity help you

What is your mental image of a woman in the first stage of labour? What does she do during contractions? We often pose these questions in one of the early classes of our antenatal groups. Many people say that they visualize her lying in bed, tossing and turning uncomfortably, breathing irregularly and rapidly, her face tense with pain and distress. And when the contraction is over? She collapses on her back, they say, and lies down, waiting for the next contraction.

What is striking about these widely held notions of the first stage of labour is that the woman is pictured *lying down*. This is probably because most births take place in hospital – and a hospital is full of beds. The automatic inference is: 'Hospital, therefore lying in bed'. This idea is strongly reinforced by almost all media images, especially in popular films and TV programmes, where childbirth is shown in passing as part of the story. In almost all of these a woman in labour is shown in exactly the way described.

Thanks to the pioneering efforts of some childbirth educators (mentioned in Chapter 1), many people are well aware that delivery itself need not occur when the mother is lying down in bed, but that there are other possibilities, such as kneeling or squatting. This is a fairly recent development; and yet it is worth mentioning that books advocating other positions still contain many pictures of women giving birth while lying on their backs. As far as the first stage is concerned, images illustrating alternatives to lying down are rare; but even where they are shown, good body use is hardly every depicted. There is a great need to change this.

It is now widely accepted that your position in relation to gravity is of the utmost importance in labour. The uterus together with its contents – baby, placenta and all – weighs over 5 kg (11 lb): this is the magnitude of the force of gravity acting upon it. If you assume the best possible position, you enlist this force to your aid. But in the worst position the same force is working against you. So the difference between the best and the worst position is over 10 kg (22 lb)! A woman adopting a disadvantageous position during labour is like a weight-lifter entering a competition with a 22 lb handicap.

Undoubtedly the worst position for a woman to adopt during contractions is lying flat on her back. This forces the uterus to work directly against gravity. Furthermore, the pressure of the contracting uterus on the large blood vessels that are now underneath it restricts the blood supply to the uterus and baby. Finally, the weight of your body on the coccyx (tail bone) hinders its movement out of the way of the baby's head.

> 'I went from 3 to 5 cm very quickly and I am convinced that this was helped by the fact that Dan finally managed to bully me off my back and onto my feet and knees.'

Any movements or positions that allow the force of gravity to aid the work of the uterus will be helpful during contractions. This includes walking, standing, sitting well on your seat bones, kneeling on all fours, and squatting. These are indeed the normal birthing positions in traditional and so-called 'primitive' societies.

It has been shown[2] that if you avoid lying down but instead choose to kneel, squat or stay upright with your torso tilted forward, you help labour in the following important ways:

- The force of gravity aids contractions and makes them stronger, more efficient and less painful.
- The curvature in your lower spine is reduced, making it easier for the baby to descend into the birth canal.
- The contracting uterus is better positioned in relation to the spine. This helps to direct the baby's head correctly in relation to your pelvis.
- The softened pelvis is allowed to widen.
- The chances of a 'good fit' of the baby are increased. For example, if the baby is in the posterior position, it is more likely to turn into the preferred anterior position. (In the posterior position your baby is lying head down but with its spine against your own spine. As a result, it needs to perform a much larger rotation.) If the baby is in the posterior position, it is encouraged to flex its neck. (The main complication of the posterior position is that the baby's neck may be extended instead of flexed, so that the head does not present its smallest circumference to the pelvic outlet. It is thought that the main cause of this complication is the mother's supine position.)

Labour pains

Most women experience considerable pain during contractions, and anticipation of this is one of the greatest anxieties that women have about childbirth.

Pain usually indicates dysfunction – 'if it hurts, something must be wrong'. A common mistake is to infer that the same applies to labour pains. This error is further compounded by the fact that labour often takes place in hospital, a place for sick people. But labour is *not* a pathological condition; it is a normal, natural process. To be sure, when there are complications, there may be an altogether different *quality* of pain, which is indeed a symptom of a disorder. In such cases medical intervention may be necessary – not only to take away the pain but, more importantly, to save the life of mother or child.

How is it, then, that such a natural process can be so painful? The theory of evolution suggests that labour pains – like most biological phenomena – are there because they serve a purpose. Indeed, there is a great deal of evidence suggesting that a certain amount of pain, far from being an unnecessary evil, is an important cue to the brain, prompting you to move in ways most appropriate for the process of labour.

In present-day Western society, pain is regarded as unacceptable. The use of painkillers and sedatives is now so widespread that they are taken as a matter of course to mask the slightest physical or mental discomfort. The more we rely on pain-killing drugs, the more difficult it will be for us to abstain from them during the intense pains of labour.

The ready availability of drugs such as pethidine and epidurals constitutes a stronger temptation than most people are prepared to admit. It also creates expectations in the minds of both carers and women in labour that they ought to be used. Self-confidence can easily be undermined by the attitude and language of carers who all too readily recommend the use of painkillers or imply that the woman would not be able to cope without taking them. A woman in one of our classes said, 'we were offered gas and air, rather as one is given sherry at a wedding reception.'

But pain-killing drugs disrupt the course of labour, upsetting the finely tuned process that has evolved over many thousands of years and making further medical intervention likely. They also have undesirable effects on both mother and baby.[3]

Not so very long ago it was common practice for women to take a variety of drugs, ranging from tobacco to thalidomide, during pregnancy. Nowadays, as the consequences have become clearer, many pregnant women are reluctant to take even the mildest drugs; education has been very effective. But attitudes to labour pains are slow to change.

Consciously or unconsciously, many women hope that by attending antenatal classes and doing certain exercises, they may achieve a pain-free labour – but even the best preparation for birth cannot guarantee this. So it is important to understand that the cyclic pains of contractions do not indicate that something is *wrong* but on the contrary that these pains are *normal and even functional,* and that we should not seek to eliminate them altogether.

> 'I did not have strong views on the type of labour and birth I wanted – my only particular desire was to avoid having an epidural if possible. As I found out more about the effects of intervention in labour, I grew more convinced that I wanted to give birth without "artificial additives". The classes helped me to feel confident by showing practical ways to cope with labour. I began to look forward positively to labour, although there were still some doubts in my mind. Could I really deal with the pain? Would the hospital intervene anyway? . . . Looking back I realize that I have been needlessly fearful. Of course labour is painful; in fact it is physically overwhelming; but it is wonderful in its own way. We seem to

be bombarded with negative images of childbirth – all I can say is that I for one found it unmissable.'

Coping with pain
By responding to pain signals with appropriate movement, you will help the course of labour and may lessen the pain.

Passivity seems to be a common cause of the failure of the uterus to contract effectively. It also intensifies the sensation of pain, creating a vicious circle: passivity → more pain → greater passivity.[4]

The value of inhibition and direction   Our instinctive reaction to pain is to freeze, which is a form of the startle reflex (see Chapter 1) and involves other symptoms of panic, such as dryness in the mouth and holding the breath. This type of reaction is functional initially when we experience severe pain: we pull away from the source of the pain (for example, a hot or sharp object) or, sometimes, we strike out. It is part of our survival mechanism; but if we hold on to tension when the immediate 'threat' has passed, continued secretion of the hormone adrenalin increases pain, and production of the body's own natural pain-relieving endorphins is blocked.[5]

This is where the process of thinking-in-activity is so important. Sometimes inhibition by itself, without any movement, helps in coping with pain.

'I began to use the Alexander Technique just to inhibit reacting to the pain. As the contractions approached I would inhibit any movement or any facial expression, any tensing against the pain, working mentally to relax into it. This calmed me right down, and although I couldn't sleep, with contractions coming every five to seven minutes, it was meditative and therefore a resting night.'

'So I was welcoming the pain into my body, thinking "I welcome you. You are bringing my baby. You are a good pain." I was going to write "loving it" but that would be too strong, and not possible, as it was the most terrible and intense pain I've ever felt. But each contraction, I knew, would only last a minute or less; the most intense part of the contraction was only ten to twenty seconds, and that fact made them bearable. "If only I can inhibit for another few seconds it will begin to die down and that will be alright."'

Giving directions can help you release any accumulated tension.

'I am on my knees holding on to the head of the bed which had been raised. The pain is all in my back and is excruciating. As the pain comes, I soften my neck and let a steady controlled breath out . . . Bernard rubs my lower back during every contraction. My contractions are now so intense, some lasting ninety seconds and more with only thirty seconds between any of them. For a while they are coming head to tail . . . A few times I feel myself begin to panic, wanting to run away. I breathe more steadily and remind myself to release. I think: I managed the last contraction and I will survive this one. I admire my body's working and try to become part of it; to fight at this stage would mean fighting myself.'

It may also be helpful to visualize what is actually happening – the shape of the contraction, dilation of the cervix, the turning of the baby's head.

'Imagining each contraction dilating the cervix and bringing me nearer to my baby I'm sure helped a lot. I also heard you saying "release the neck".'

Softening your mouth   Instead of meeting contractions with resistance and tension, when your body signals to you that a contraction is about to begin, let your neck be free and breathe out softly through an open, soft and wet mouth. The mouth, the eyelids, the vagina and the anus are controlled by sphincteral muscles, which tend to work together. (You can confirm this by shutting your eyes tight, and observing what happens to your other sphincters.) Relaxing the mouth helps to relax the vagina; this, in turn, releases pressure on the cervix.

By deliberately producing saliva you may be able to help this process. A dry mouth is associated with tension and panic, a wet mouth with a more relaxed state. (For example, copious salivation can be triggered by sexual orgasm.) Producing saliva may be a way of sending a 'relax' signal to your brain. You can encourage salivation by smiling or even by thinking about smiling.

'Each time I felt [a contraction] coming I called Clive to be with me . . . He encouraged me to see my cervix opening up as the roses were. He also . . . reminded me to keep my mouth moist, though I remembered to do this myself.'

Breathing naturally   With your neck free and your back lengthening and widening, your breathing will regulate itself, creating a proper exchange of oxygen and carbon dioxide. Do not attempt to take deep breaths; if you over-inflate your lungs, you reduce the exchange of gases rather than increasing it.

If for any reason the rhythm of your labour falters and you hyperventilate (breathe in and out rapidly), you lose carbon dioxide too fast. This may result in unpleasant sensations such as dizziness. In extreme cases it may cause fainting and foetal distress. A good way of dealing with this is to cup your hands over your nose and mouth and breathe in your own exhaled air. You can also use a paper bag for this purpose. Also, your partner can help you to re-establish your breathing rhythm and calm you down by breathing gently and rhythmically close to your face.

'I breathe during contractions, blowing out through soft, wet lips, concentrating on the out-breath; but find I over-ventilate. So I just concentrate on observing my breathing, which deepens naturally and, in the strongest contractions, takes my concentration deeply within myself – an extraordinary experience.'

Movement during contractions

'Perhaps the most apt way is to say that what you taught me in our
Alexander lessons was the basis for everything that I did. After my
labour was over Ben described you as the absent midwife, and that about
sums it up. Sharon, the midwife, was impressed by the fact that we were
calm, knew what we were doing and got on with it . . . I was coping with
the pain either by leaning against Ben and moving from side to side with
him, or by getting onto all fours and then doing the pear movement.
Ben's hands were on my back and shoulders, and I kept thinking about
directions.'

We shall now describe a few basic movements and some variations. In
our experience, these movements can be particularly effective during
contractions in the first stage of labour. They enable you to take advantage of the force of gravity while you are maintaining a good neck-head-
back relationship. They also help you cope with the pain by going along
with it rather than trying to fight it (which only makes it worse); in
this way you encourage your body to produce its own pain-relieving
endorphins.

It cannot be repeated often enough: what makes a difference is not so
much *what* you do but *how* you do it. The point is not merely to stay
upright or kneel or squat, but *to maintain good coordination while doing so*.
Try to avoid impulsive and jerky movement and remind yourself to
'think-in-activity'.

'Now I was very restricted in movement. My right hand had the drip into
the vein and it was very uncomfortable so I couldn't use it at all. . . . From
my left were the monitors – the contractions monitor and the baby's
heartbeat monitor – both belted to my bump. So I could sit, lie or kneel
up on the bed, or, as I discovered, lean forwards over a bean-bag or the
shoulders of someone sitting on the bed end. . . . Although I used all the
above positions, I wasn't moving once in them. . . . So again my tools for
the labour were inhibition, breathing, positive thinking and visualization,
and the helpers with me.'

Labour, as the word itself suggests, is hard work. For the first-time
mother, the initial phase of dilation may proceed so slowly that she may
come close to despair. Will the pain ever ease? She will need a lot of support and encouragement from her partner and carers. Then, as the first
stage progresses, she may undergo a psychological transformation and
regain confidence, entering a 'deeper level of consciousness'.[6]

'At this stage I was totally withdrawn even from Nic. There was always
this nagging little voice in my head saying that this was awful and I was
going to have to take something for the pain. I could barely talk to
anyone and just paced up and down the small room as if obsessed . . .
Being totally vertical was the only comfortable position. The bean-bag
was useless. I just paced up and down without stopping . . . Suddenly I
felt totally elated. I was excited because I knew we were getting there and

I was completely in control of what was happening. Now I was having gaps between the contractions and could even tell Nic I loved him, which was wonderful. There was a great sense of opening up emotionally as well as physically.'

'I found that squatting was the most comfortable position during contractions at that point . . . I managed for the rest of the labour to be either squatting or standing, supported by James. I kept on having flashes of images from Michel Odent's film – they gave me great reassurance, that such an overpowering and fast experience was completely natural. Apparently the contractions were so strong much of the time that they went off the top of the monitor's graph paper! . . . In a weird kind of way the pain itself was seductive.'

All the movements we shall describe can be performed both at home and in hospital, on the floor or on a bed. Some of them are for you alone; others may be done either with or without a partner; sometimes a partner's help may be invaluable.

Even if you intend to have your baby in hospital, there is usually no need to rush there. You can spend a good part of the first stage at home. Prepare a comfortable room with plenty of cushions on the floor. A bean-bag or a gymnastic ball can be very helpful. You will also need a chair – a simple kitchen chair with a back rest will do.

When you do get to hospital, make sure the furniture is arranged to your liking in the labour room. Many people do not realize they can ask to have things moved or changed.

Varying your movement   During the whole period of dilation it is helpful to vary your movements and positions. You may feel the need to do so because in each position or movement you use your muscles in different ways and variation prevents tiredness and strain. You will find, at different times, that this or that movement feels more 'right' and comfortable, depending on the phase in the cycle of contractions, the strength of the contraction and the degree to which labour has advanced. Sometimes you may want to move vigorously; at other times you hardly move at all.

'I would like to add how very valuable I found the practice movements. And when the contractions became very intense I could hear you saying "Don't get stuck only in one position" and moved from all fours to a half squat, which was wonderful for times when there was more downward pressure.'

Varying your movements also helps to advance labour. An important function of movement is to 'jog' the baby into place, encouraging it to fit snugly into your pelvis and birth canal. Since the initial position of the baby and the shape of the mother's pelvis vary considerably, it is impossible to tell in advance which movements will be most effective, and so it is a good idea to experiment.

Try altering position *between* contractions, as it may be very difficult to change during the contraction itself. For example, if at the beginning of a

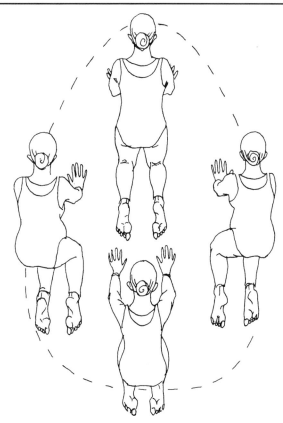

Drawing 10 The 'pear' movement.

contraction you are kneeling on all fours, then you may not be able to get up on your feet until the contraction is over.

To get the most benefit from the following movements, you need to become familiar with them before you go into labour. It is a good idea to practise them thoroughly during the last few months of your pregnancy. Study the text and the illustrations carefully; then ask your partner or a friend to read the descriptions of the movements to you while you try them out. (You can also pre-record them on tape.) Practise the movements slowly and gently – there is no need to rush.

The 'pear' movement   Kneel on all fours. Move your torso slowly backwards and forwards, keeping your neck free and your back long, making sure that your lower back does not hollow and collapse. The pivots of the movements are the wrists, the knees and the hip joints; your elbows and shoulders shouldn't be locked; the pelvis shouldn't be tilted (either up-and-down or from side to side) but should retain its normal alignment with the spine. Your torso remains roughly parallel to the floor. You can vary this movement: for example, you may add to the backwards and forwards movement a simultaneous sideways movement, resulting in a

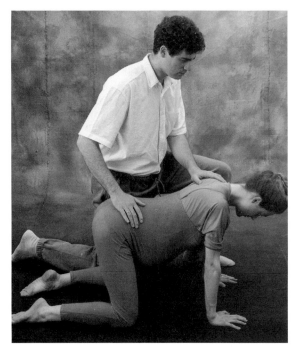

Fig. 110 The pear movement with help of a partner.

Fig. 111 Releasing tension after a contraction.

rotation of the torso (see Drawing 10). Your head traces an oval in the same plane as the back. (The longer axis of the oval is an extension of the spine and the shorter axis is parallel to the shoulder girdle.) Imagine: if you held a long pencil in your mouth, it would draw a pear-shape on the floor.

Your partner can participate by laying his hands on your back and moving with you (Fig. 110). When the contraction is over, sit on your heels and rest one arm on your partner (Fig. 111). After a contraction, releasing tension in your neck and shoulders is of enormous help in regaining your composure and restoring normal breathing.

In early labour, the pear movement can be soothing. While doing it, breathe out through a soft wet mouth. When the pain intensifies, you will probably want to move more vigorously. Allow your elbows and knees to bend so that your torso is closer to the floor (remaining roughly parallel to it) and your sitting bones approach your heels.

'With each contraction, I started doing the "pear" movement, which did help me to relax into the pain; but I felt I was using up too much energy. After a while I realized that if I consciously released my neck just before the pain hit me – just as soon as I sensed the contraction coming – it became a lot easier.'

Your partner can sometimes move with you, while at other times he may support your head, making it easier for you to keep your neck aligned with your spine.

Several variations of this movement are possible and can be used according to your needs.

Using a gymnastic ball   The gymnastic ball is a surprisingly useful prop in labour. Its firm yet springy surface, and rolling motion, are exactly what you need. The pear movement is particularly pleasant when done with your arms, head and chest resting on the ball (Figs 112, 113). The support provided by the ball makes it easier for you to move in a relaxed way and keep your directions going.

Using a chair   Instead of kneeling on all fours, you can perform the pear movement with your head and arms resting on a bean-bag, a large cushion or a chair (Fig. 114).

Squatting using a door   This movement, as described on p. 76, may also help you cope better with the pain of contractions. Squatting is often associated with the second stage of labour, but many women discover that it is very useful throughout. Using the door handles for support, you may find it soothing to swing the door gently and rock rhythmically from side to side. When the contraction is over, you can either get up or lower yourself to kneeling in order to rest.

Instead of using a door, you can ask your partner to help support your weight. In this case it is best for him to stand in a 'monkey' and sway

Fig. 112

Fig. 113

Figs 112–113   The pear movement using a gym ball.

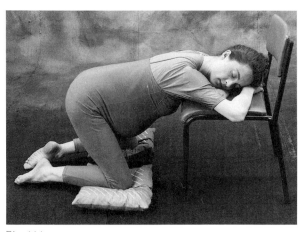

Fig. 114

Fig. 115

Fig. 116

Rocking during a squat.

from side to side in time with you. In this way he can protect his own back from injury, and you will be confident that he is able to support you easily. When the contraction is over, he can help you get up by taking a step back while lifting you.

Rocking during a squat   From a squatting position, place your hands flat on the floor in front of you (Fig. 115). With your head leading, shift your weight over on to your hands while keeping the elbows flexed so as not to create tension in your shoulders. Rock back and forth (Fig. 116).

Moving in a half-squat   If you find full squatting too difficult, you can perform a similar rocking movement while kneeling on one knee.
   From kneeling on both knees, bring one foot forward and slightly to the side. With your head leading, lunge forward. You can extend this movement further forwards and backwards, so that in the extreme forward position your palms touch the floor and take some of your weight, and in the extreme backward position you will be sitting on your heel.

Fig. 117   Fig. 118

Monkey with a partner.

From time to time alternate between left and right. You can vary the movement in other ways. For example, if you are sitting on your right heel, you can bring your left foot closer to your bottom, and as you lunge forward your left side may rest on your thigh. Also, your partner can move with you.

Movements based on monkey and lunge   Like squatting and kneeling, being on your feet is advantageous during labour. The forward tilt of the torso in both monkey and lunge is helpful in facilitating the labour process.

> 'As the contractions get stronger, my overwhelming response is to push the pelvis forward, closing off the hips and causing pressure on my lower back. I am afraid that it will be really painful if I bend at the hips. I have to inhibit strongly and encourage myself to lean forward and bend in my knees and hips ["monkey"]. Once having achieved this I am amazed; the pain lessens, the tummy is suspended forward in its hammock of muscles and the activity of the contraction seems to be intensified and localized in the abdomen. Even so, with each stronger contraction it is a battle for me between what I want to do (tighten) and what I know will work better for me (free off the hips).'

These movements are especially useful if your baby is in the posterior position. (This is not uncommon: about half of all babies are in the

Fig. 119

Fig. 120

Monkey with a partner (close together).

Fig. 121 Monkey – partner standing behind.

posterior position at the onset of labour.) As we have mentioned, there is evidence that movements based on the monkey and lunge encourage the posterior-position baby to turn into the preferred anterior position and to flex its head.[7]

Most of the following movements involve your partner, so it is best to practise them together in order to coordinate your actions.

'Monkey' with a partner – first variation   Stand facing your partner, both of you in the monkey position, with your arms on each other's shoulders (Fig. 117). During a contraction, sway gently from side to side, transferring your weight from one bent leg to the other (Fig. 118). While moving, remember to give yourself directions: the head leads and the torso follows, the back lengthens and widens. The movement hinges on the leg joints: there is no wriggling or unnecessary tilting of the pelvis. Do not tighten your buttocks. Keep the soles of your feet in firm contact with the floor and aim to move in time with each other.

'Monkey' with a partner – second variation   You can combine swaying from side to side with an up-and-down movement, as a result of which your head describes an oval shape. (This is in fact the 'pear' movement done in the 'monkey' position.)

'Monkey' with a partner – third variation   If you feel that you need more support, get closer to your partner, put your arms round his shoulders and let him hug you (Figs. 119, 120).

'Monkey' with a partner – fourth variation   Alternatively, your partner can stand behind you, perhaps supporting your abdomen, both of you in the monkey position (Fig. 121). He can also stimulate your nipples, which encourages the secretion of oxytocin.

'Monkey' with a partner – fifth variation   In this variation, you adopt a deeper monkey position. In order to support your weight, your partner has to sit on a chair (Figs. 122, 123). He can rest or perhaps give you a back massage.

Lunging with a partner   In this movement – as in those based on monkey – you transfer your weight from one foot to the other; but instead of swaying from side to side, you move back and forth. The rhythm of this movement requires well-rehearsed coordination between you and your partner: as you lunge forward and transfer your weight on to the foot in front, he moves back and transfers his weight on to his back foot. You can move at arm's length from each other (Fig. 124). Or, if you need to support more of your weight on him, move closer together (Fig. 125).

> 'The lunging "position" is so powerful [during contractions] . . . There is such a sensation of lull when the contraction dies. It's so important to get to the centre of the pain – the vortex of the whirlpool is how I envisaged it. The mind does this for you and the body responds in terms of movement which may well be violent. The movements are erotic, like

Fig. 122

Fig. 123

Monkey – partner sitting on chair.

Fig. 124 Lunging with partner.

Fig. 125 Lunging with partner (close together).

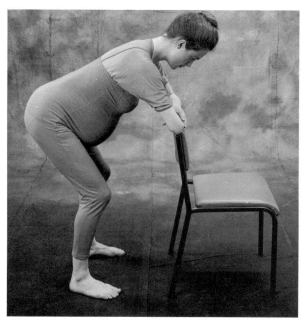

Fig. 126   Monkey (leaning on chair).

making love. In fact when your partner is close and is "dancing" with you one could perhaps be deceived. Erotic, sexual but not – for me anyway – orgasmic! I do believe that a woman has to be confident in her body to be able to let go like that . . . We have to trust in the power of our bodies. They function unaided in the most marvellous way if we allow ourselves to be taught.'

'Monkey' and lunge on your own   Instead of supporting your weight on a partner, you can use a piece of furniture (Fig. 126) or a wall.

Creating your own variations   Use your understanding of the Alexander Technique to be creative: you will probably invent further variations on the basic themes and perhaps even new movements.

If at some point you cannot or do not wish to move much during a contraction, adopt any of the positions we have described. If you are not on all fours let your torso tilt forward, pivoting over your hip joints. For example, if you are sitting, lean forward and support yourself on your partner or a piece of furniture. Aim to maintain an expanded, released posture; focus on breathing out, to prevent holding your breath.

F.M. Alexander noted:

I have found that in this process of acquiring a conscious direction of use my pupils gradually develop a higher standard of sensory awareness or appreciation of what they are doing in the use of themselves so that when it comes to carrying out a course of activity they possess a criterion within themselves which will enable them to judge whether the use they are employing is right or not for the purpose.[8]

He stressed that this acquired skill is of particular value in 'reactions to the stimulus of the unfamiliar'.

Using the time between contractions

The first stage of labour can be prolonged, and you will need to conserve your energy and to keep a balance between rest and activity. Don't forget to drink and eat (see Appendix 1); and remember to empty your bladder frequently.

Between contractions, give yourself an occasional rest, or engage in some gentle activity. In early labour you may, for example, wish to go for a walk.

> 'My sister came round and together we started to pace the streets of West Hampstead. I remember that walk so clearly and I expect I always will. We must have walked miles and miles, and talked and talked. It was a lovely warm evening and even West Hampstead looked pretty . . . By the time we were nearing home I had begun to have real contractions – nothing too painful but I knew they were there. When we got home, my sister (who is a midwife) suggested that we got the bedroom ready . . . I then had a bath and the doctor arrived. It was, or seemed to me, terribly unreal: we all sat in the sitting room – the doctor, me, my sister and my husband drinking coffee.'

Later on you may not feel like walking; crawling, as described on pp. 66–9, can then enhance active relaxation. If you are at home, you are free to use all the space available. In hospital a mat will be useful (and it is therefore a good idea to bring one with you, in case the hospital cannot supply one).

As your labour progresses, your need for rest will be greater. Re-read the passages on 'resting' on pp. 79–80; most of what was said there applies equally to relaxation between contractions.

You can rest on a gymnastic ball, bean-bag or chair; you may lie on your side or in the child position. The advantage of the gym ball is that its mobility keeps your muscles in tone while you are resting.

If you rest seated, incline your torso forward a little and lean on your partner or on a piece of furniture. This makes it easier for you to maintain your neck-head-back relationship and to lengthen your back. Alternatively, you may prefer to sit astride a kitchen chair, facing its back and leaning on it. When seated, the pressure on your seat bones encourages the outlet of your pelvis to widen.

If you choose to rest lying down, you may be lucky and snatch a refreshing catnap. While you are resting, you may like your partner to give you a massage.

Massage

In many cultures massage is used during pregnancy and childbirth. It is also recommended by most modern advocates of natural childbirth, who suggest that regular body massage by your partner during pregnancy –

apart from showing tenderness, love and care – also helps to create a bond between father and baby.[9]

Although massage is not part of the Alexander Technique, it can be combined with the movements recommended in this book, as a further means of releasing tension.

When your partner massages you, he should pay attention to his own body and use it as well as he can: good massage is given by the entire body, not just by the hands. His hands will be more alive when their movement is part of the general movement of his body. He should be careful not to strain his back. The monkey or lunge – with his feet wide apart – will enable him to move flexibly and prevent strain and fatigue. If he is working on the floor, he will be more comfortable – and therefore able to give you a better massage – if he sits or kneels on a cushion, bending from his hip joints and knees, not from his back.

You may like oil to be applied during the massage. Special aromatic oil mixtures are sometimes recommended for use during pregnancy and labour and are available in pharmacies, but any good body lotion or oil will do. The aroma of the oil creates a more personal atmosphere and overcomes surrounding clinical odours; and it is also believed by many to have special healing properties.

During contractions, you may feel like having your legs rubbed vigorously. In order to help the blood circulation, the up strokes should use more pressure, whereas the down strokes should be lighter, perhaps done with the back of the hand. Many women enjoy some pressure being applied to their lower back and sacrum during contractions. The pressure should be provided mainly by the weight of your partner's body, rather than by straining the muscles of his arms; his hands should stay relaxed.

Between contractions, the massage can be gentler, to aid relaxation (Fig. 127). If the massage helps you doze for a minute or two, all the better.

Using a handball for massage is surprisingly pleasant and soothing (Fig. 128). Your partner can roll the ball in a circular motion, starting (say) with your left foot. Then he rolls and circles the ball up your left leg, then on to your buttocks, along the spine. The pressure can be varied, but it is best not to exert too much pressure on the spine. The ball can then be rolled over your left shoulder and arm, all the way to your left palm, helping it to open. He can then start with your right foot.

> 'We went into the living room – I no longer felt like sitting on the chair, but knelt on all fours, sometimes resting my head on a large floor-cushion. Graham used a football to massage my back and feet when I was resting on my haunches and he put on [a recording of] Thomas Tallis's *Spem in Alium*.'

You may not like to have your body massaged, but perhaps massaging your feet will make you feel good. Even in a well-heated room, your feet may be rather cold, and massage will warm them up.

Alternatively, a simple light touch of your partner's hand may be all

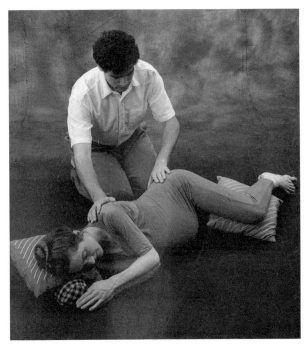

Fig. 127 A gentle massage.

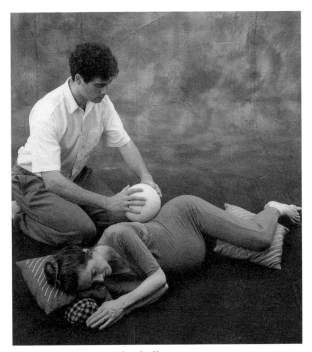

Fig. 128 Massage with a ball.

you want. A cool hand on the back of your neck can be very relaxing, although some women do not wish to be touched at all.

> 'I also needed hands on me: if I was left to do the most intense part of the contraction without hands on me I felt abandoned, even though they were in the room; it was as though they didn't care, didn't understand.'

Using Water in Labour

Largely due to the ideas of Michel Odent,[10] immersion in water during labour has recently attracted growing interest. Even before this had become fashionable, many women used their own baths or showers as aids to relaxation: immersion in water at body temperature has a soothing effect and there is some evidence that it encourages the progress of labour. The advantage of a small pool over an ordinary bath is that it allows you greater freedom of movement. In recent years many hospitals have introduced special pools into their labour wards. For a home birth, a portable birthing pool can be hired privately.

If you use a pool, any benefits from it will be all the greater if you use yourself well; good use of the body is as important in water as it is on dry land. Take care to avoid jerky movements, especially over-arching of your lumbar area and twisting your spine.

Some of the movements we have described here can be performed while you are partly immersed; in fact, kneeling and squatting become easier.

Transition

The transition from the first stage of labour to the second is not sharply defined and can take a great variety of forms. You may not experience any clear transitional phase, but suddenly feel an irresistible, instinctive urge to bear down almost as soon as your cervix is fully dilated. On the other hand, there may be a lull between the end of dilation and the onset of this urge.

In recent years it has been recognized that a transitional lull is not necessarily a sign that something is wrong. There is no need to advise the woman to push before the instinctive urge to do so has become irresistible. (Such intervention may be compared to trying to force a bowel movement by straining before the bowel opens spontaneously by reflex action.)

If you experience a transitional lull – let it be a peaceful interlude. Take it easy and rest, inclining your torso slightly forward on a chair or a large bean bag or, better still, use a gymnastic ball (shown earlier). Enjoy the gentle rolling motion.

> 'There was a lull in the contractions. I leaned on the stool and felt sleepy, relaxed, peaceful and happy. Then came the unmistakable urge to push.'

A common experience is that of a dramatic physical and emotional change as dilation is about to reach its climax. At this point, contractions are more intense and closer together: sometimes you will have two or three contractions with hardly a breathing space between them. This may be accompanied by shaking or even vomiting. The emotional changes can be quite bizarre and manifest themselves in uncharacteristic behaviour. Women have been known to start dressing and say that they have had enough and want to go home; others become easily upset or very angry; yet others start groaning in a way that surprises them.

You may get a premature urge to bear down. This is most likely if the baby was in the posterior position and is now completing its rotation, exerting pressure on your rectum. Another quite common cause is an anterior lip: your cervix has dilated unevenly, leaving a 'lip' or fold of skin, in front of the baby's head.

You can tell that the urge to bear down is premature, if it is not impossible to resist. In this case, bearing down may bruise the cervix.

'At about 1 p.m. I got a terrible urge to push. Phyllis examined me again but I was only 9.5 cm. I found this period very difficult. Clive knelt in front of me, I was kneeling on all fours on the bed. . . . I tried lying on my side to ease the urge to push but this hurt too much.'

'The transition stage seemed to last for ever; however it was only about thirty minutes. I felt very cold at this point, even though I was sweating a lot, and my legs began to shake.'

Body use during transition

All the movements that we have described for first-stage contractions can also be of great help during transition. When you are in labour you will find whichever of them is appropriate to your own circumstances. Now we would like to mention three additional techniques that are especially relevant to transition.

Whispered and vocalized 'ah'   It is here that you can make good use of your whispered 'ah' practice (see pp. 52 and 80). You may also add vocalization, so that the 'ah' is voiced or even shouted rather than whispered. This is a good way of groaning in style, and without damaging your throat and vocal cords.

'Making a sound was invaluable and I found a deep low sound helped tremendously – also to keep my lips loose.'

'I remembered the advice not to worry about any moans and groans you make (as long as you are not wasting energy screaming) – that is quite liberating, as in England traditionally people are encouraged to "grin and bear it". I certainly exercised my voice that day!

Breathing   If you get a premature urge to bear down, you can help yourself to overcome it by shallow puffing through a soft wet mouth, as if you are trying to blow out many candles one by one. Do not let your head jump in the direction in which you blow, but keep your neck free – jerky head movements will make you tired and tense. Don't worry about the in-breaths – these will take care of themselves. If, between puffs, you do not tense up but release the muscles used in blowing out, your intake of air will automatically be sufficient for the next puff, so that you can go on puffing without getting short of breath.

The knee-chest position   If you have an anterior lip the best position to assume during a contraction is the knee-chest (Fig. 85). At the same time breathe gently with a shallow puffing as described previously.

When the contraction is over, sit on your heels or change to a squat or half-squat. Altering your position in this way has the effect of easing the pressure on the cervix during contractions and increasing it between them. As a result, the lip can disappear. (If a midwife finds a lip during examination, she may smooth it manually.)

The knee-chest position can also be helpful in counteracting the premature urge to bear down and in slowing down a very fast labour.

> 'When I was 7 cm dilated I had an anterior lip and tremendous urge to push, and automatically took the head-down, bottom-up position.'

Encouragement and reassurance – 'you're nearly there!' – by your partner and others around you can help you to sail through a difficult transition, and is uplifting in a physical sense too – a negative attitude can pull you down. You may prefer your partner to help you conjure up peaceful images, particularly of flowing water. On the other hand, you may want to hear descriptions of what is happening inside you. Laughter at this time can be a wonderful tonic; if your partner or midwife can make you

Opposite: These drawings show three phases in the second stage of labour. In the first of these, the baby's head is just visible through the birth canal. The second shows the baby's head 'crowning': it is at the point of freeing itself and being born. In the third, the baby's shoulders are emerging.

You can follow the progress of the birth by drawing an imaginary straight line between the top of the mother's pelvis and the bottom end of her pubic bone. In the first drawing the head is beginning to pivot. In the second, the head is almost free of the pelvic bones and continues to pivot; the back of the head arches over the mother's pubic bone.

During the first stage of labour the baby was facing towards the mother's side but by now it has turned to face her back.

Because the vagina is not directly under the pelvic brim but is inclined to it almost at a right angle, the baby needs to perform a movement of going round a bend, somewhat like a foot going into a boot.

Once the head has freed itself, it rotates again through about 90 degrees so that once more it is facing to one side. The body rotates following the head. First one shoulder comes out (see third drawing), then the other.

Notice how the mother's coccyx moves out of the way to create a wider passage. The top of the uterus continues to retract downwards and towards the spine.

When the baby's head is about to be born, the vagina stretches to let it through.

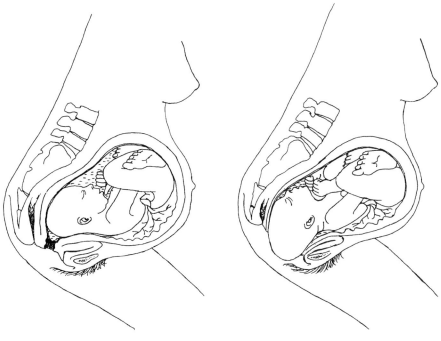

Drawing 11   *Drawing 12*

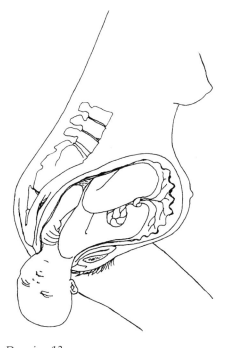

Drawing 13

laugh, you are really lucky. However, if you prefer them to keep quiet, do not hesitate to tell them so.

'I raised my head and looked Brian in the eyes. I said, "Brian, I cannot go on any longer; isn't there any other way of doing it?" What I meant was, I need help; perhaps they are going to suggest a Caesarean – which seemed a good idea at the time. Everyone fell silent. Then Brian said, "We could have adopted, but it's a bit too late now." They all burst out laughing. I wasn't sure about the joke, but I found myself joining in. Half an hour later our daughter was born.'

The Second Stage

The urge to bear down is triggered off by the baby's head pressing against your pelvic floor. This stimulates special nerve endings in your perineum to send a message to the pituitary gland in the base of your brain. The gland releases through the bloodstream a hormonal message to the uterus, creating an irresistible urge to bear down.

Again, several synchronized processes are set in motion. The uterus continues to contract and now it also retracts rapidly. At the same time the baby's head begins to travel down through the birth canal. Its neck begins to extend; the head pivots and as it is born it also rotates, allowing the shoulders to emerge after it.

The duration of the second stage can vary from a few minutes to a few hours.

'The last two or three contractions before we got to the labour room were heavy, grunting ones, which frightened Dan but in fact were more bearable than the first-stage ones. In fact, that is what surprised me about my labour: the second stage was almost enjoyable compared with the first stage. Luckily I dilated well and did not have to resist the urge to push, so was able to give in totally to the reflex. Only about an hour and a half after we arrived at the labour room, Tycho catapulted onto the bed.'

'My second stage lasted just twelve minutes and the midwives were wonderfully encouraging. Still shocked and dazed, my new 6 lb daughter was gently placed in my arms. Neither she nor I cried. We just peered curiously at each other and said a calm, silent "hello".'

The change in your hormonal balance prepares you for bearing down: you may feel a surge of energy, due to the higher level of adrenalin in your bloodstream. The nature of the contractions also changes: they are likely to be more widely spaced and the urge to bear down may be felt several times during each contraction. Be prepared for a stinging or burning sensation (which may be followed by numbness) as the vaginal muscles are stretched by the baby's head.

'The midwife tells me when to push and when to stop and we gently ease the head out. The head circumference is big and his passage tears me slightly inside my vagina – an unpleasant burning sensation – but the head is born with the perineum intact. The rest is born easily. He is a big boy and he is really ugly!'

Body use during the second stage

In addition to facilitating the labour process and coping with pain, good use of your body can also prevent or minimize tears in your perineum.

By gaining awareness of the working of your body, you will be able to understand its signals and respond to them. You will be more likely to allow the bearing down to happen spontaneously.

'Eventually I was fully dilated and the baby had turned. Now they let me push in earnest, exhorting me furiously, often not in tune with the actual contractions: wanting me to start too soon and go on after the contraction had gone. And this made them less effective. Really there should have been encouragement to inhibit pushing and just go with it when it happened – which I tried to do a bit, despite their shouting, as I found it was more effective. I managed a few good pushes, by ignoring them and inhibiting, I think, and the baby appeared down the birth canal.'

'I had the confidence to push long before the midwife thought it was time to do so. It must have been right, as Stephen was a large baby (9 lb 3 oz) with a very large head and I did not tear as he was born. His head kept popping out and slipping back between contractions for quite a while; but he finally emerged, perfect. He hardly cried at all and seemed very calm. I felt elated, had only one stitch, and was able to take a shower and sit comfortably straight away.'

Movement during bearing down   Elizabeth Noble, a leading American childbirth educator and physiotherapist, points out:

Squatting . . . offers one of the most functional positions for birth. According to studies in Sweden by Dr Christian Ehrstrom, when a mother squats the pelvic outlet is at its widest, increased by one to two centimetres . . . The contraction of the abdominal muscles is very efficient in squatting as they are in a shortened middle position of their range. Not only does gravity provide additional force from above, but there is no counterforce from below. The vagina becomes shorter and wider, and less effort is required by the mother to open up and let the baby out at her own pace . . . Women who squat for birth can generally deliver their babies without any manual assistance at all. Gravity and the free space around the perineum allow the baby's rotation manoeuvres to be accomplished spontaneously.[11]

To this we would like to add that in order to take best advantage of the force of gravity, your birth canal should be pointing downwards. This means that the preferred positions are those in which your torso is *tilted well forwards*. For example, if you are squatting, avoid a full squat with an upright torso: this exerts too much pressure on the pelvic floor and increases the risk of tearing. Tilt forward so that your outlet faces down-

Fig. 129   *Fig. 130*

Supported squat.

wards, and hold on to something or someone.

Squatting can take a variety of forms: from a deep 'monkey' to a full squat. Your partner can be of great help by supporting your squat. You can face him and support yourself around his neck, or he can stand behind you and hold you under your arms. In either case he must protect his own back by adopting the 'monkey' himself (Fig. 129, 130). Alternatively, you can support yourself on the shoulders of your partner and a friend on either side.

Many Western women find some form of kneeling easier than squatting. If you prefer, kneel on the floor, with your partner sitting on a chair in front of you, enabling you to support the upper part of your body on his knees (Drawing 14). If you kneel on a bed, you can support yourself on the headboard; or, keeping close to its edge, you can put your arms around your partner's shoulders.

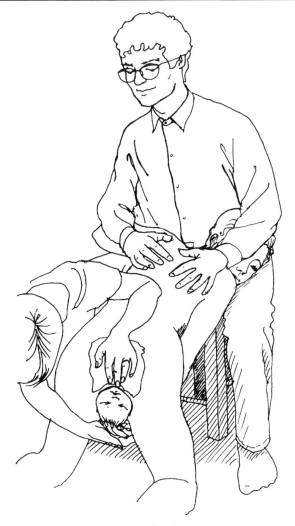

Drawing 14 Kneeling to give birth.

If you are on all fours (whether on the floor or on a bed), you can use the help of two people to provide a counterforce while you are bearing down (Fig. 131).

It is a good idea to practise these movements with your partner well in advance

'When I reach the birthing room I [find out] that the heartbeat of the baby is fine and the head is already on the perineum. At this point I completely hand over my authority to the midwives and doctor. For the first time I am not in charge and I'm lying on my back. The contractions subside and I no longer have the desire to push. Several times I ask if I can go on all fours and I am gently dissuaded – the midwives will not be able to see

Fig. 131   Kneeling supported by two people.

properly. I am urged to push but really I can't even feel the contractions or desire any more. The midwives are amazed at my apparent difficulty. I have a short rest and then decide to take charge again. I insist on going on all fours. The contractions immediately start up strongly; once again I notice how the activity is localized around my abdomen. I can now push; I feel the contractions working and the resistance of the baby to push against – I know we are on our way.'

'For the second-stage labour I was on all fours on the bed, with a heap of pillows to rest my head on. Antony helped by wiping my forehead and face with a wet flannel. The contractions I had felt in first stage had stopped. I remember this stage as quite long periods of calm, interrupted by the most almighty contraction of my body as it tried to push Stephanie out. I describe it like this on purpose as the pushing force did not seem consciously induced; I could also not help but verbally express the pushing-out feeling. I was concerned at this point not to allow any one push to be too strong or too quick, which might cause me to tear, and was therefore trying desperately to keep some degree of control. I do not know how many "pushes" there were in all, but I do recall that after each of the last few I really thought she was out and was surprised to find she wasn't. However, she finally came out at 7.57 a.m. a perfect baby girl.'

'There was nothing I could do not to push: the urge was so strong, so compulsive. I was on my knees, with my arms around my husband. I could feel the head moving down almost as if its own weight controlled its slow movement to be born. I tried to relax and let it happen with softness. I went on to all fours – the cord was around the baby's neck, tightly. "Don't push!" Frantic panic on my part – oh baby, my baby – I must do everything I am told not to hurt the baby. "Now, one big push, as hard as you can." She cried; I knew she was alive. "Can I pick her up?" (I haven't really put her down since.) Gradually her colour came.'

'The baby was delivered with me half-standing, leaning against Ben. Sharon [the midwife] was dabbing cold antiseptic on my piles (the gory details) which was great because they were bad. Because I was leaning against Ben he could feel the baby coming out. Pushing him out was an extraordinary emotional experience for me, which is impossible to describe.'

Releasing *up* to bear *down!* As we have already mentioned, the urge to bear down during the second stage is involuntary and because of this it is difficult to practise in advance. The best you can do is to prepare for it mentally and understand the process, so that when the time comes you know how to react to the signals of your body.

Bearing down does *not* mean pulling yourself down. On the contrary, it is best done by allowing your head to go forward and up, and your back to lengthen, in opposition to the bearing-down force. (In many 'primitive' societies the woman achieves this by hanging on to some object or a rope.) Visualize the two heads – your own and your baby's – moving away from each other.

Most of the work is done by the involuntary action of your uterus. To help it along, breathe out freely; avoid holding your breath and don't strain. As you breathe out, feel free to vocalize, even shout. Here again your practice of the whispered and vocalized 'ah' should prove its value. To protect your vocal cords as well as relax your vagina, keep your voice to its deepest pitch: allow yourself to moan and groan rather than shriek.

As the baby's head begins to emerge, the pelvic floor muscles have to stretch. By breathing out freely, through a wide open mouth, you allow them to relax and stretch more effectively, minimizing damage to the perineum.

'The urge to open my bowels was almost uncontrollable and I screamed "I really have to shit!". When the doctor examined me he told me I was fully dilated . . . and I could push the baby out. I said "I need to sit up". Chris helped me into a kneeling position leaning against him. I pushed and the pain was unbelievable. The midwife said "Don't scream when you push, you are tensing; relax and push or you will tear". I managed to stop screaming and concentrated on pushing . . . When I stopped screaming the pain was less bad; I had obviously been trying to hold back subconsciously.'

'I could not believe it. Three hours in labour and not even a single tear. I am sure this was thanks to the advice to rub almond oil into my perineum which we'd been doing for about six weeks prior.'*

*We should point out that this practice is not part of the Alexander Technique, but one which is often found helpful. Any suitable oil can be used.

'As the contractions became stronger I became less inhibited and gave full vent to my vocal cords. . . . I faced the wall and grabbed the end of the bed whilst in a kneeling position. I had one contraction and then my waters broke with considerable force. After two or three contractions and a lot of noise from me I put my hand down between my legs and felt the baby's head.'

The Third Stage

The third stage of labour begins from the moment the baby is born and ends with the expulsion of the placenta and membranes from the uterus. It may last from a few minutes to half an hour or more. Again, several processes take place simultaneously. We shall first describe the natural, physiological course of the third stage.

After the baby is born, the uterus contracts and retracts rapidly. When the area to which the placenta is attached is reduced to about half its original size, the placenta begins to peel off, first at the middle and then at the rim. At this point the placenta takes the shape of a big closed flower, with the umbilical cord as the stem.

As the placenta peels off, the mother's blood inside it is squeezed back into the connecting veins in the wall of the uterus. As these veins become congested, they are ruptured and their torn ends are sealed off by the surrounding muscles of the uterus, which act as 'living ligatures', so that the mother's loss of blood is normally quite small. (Usually the small amount of lost blood is contained in the 'closed flower' of the placenta.)

While all this is happening, the umbilical cord continues to pulsate and pumps blood into the baby from the placenta, which shrinks further as a result. The detached placenta now falls into the lower part of the uterus, pulling the membranes with it.

A managed third stage

In most Western countries it is now virtually standard procedure to give the mother an injection of syntometrine, as the first shoulder of the baby emerges. This is done in order to reduce the risk of haemorrhage by speeding up the expulsion of the placenta. The desirability of this procedure is still the subject of some controversy because of its possible side effects.[12]

It is extremely important not to confuse the managed process of the third stage with the natural physiological process, because your own role in each is quite different.

If you accept syntometrine, it is best for you to lie down during the third stage. The cord must be clamped and cut immediately after the baby is born and the placenta is gently pulled out by the midwife or doctor; this is done most safely if you are lying down. However, you need not be passive and collapsed. Give yourself directions and breathe normally.

Fig. 132 Breastfeeding.

Body use during a natural third stage

It is important to stay upright, with your torso tilted forward. The placenta may then simply fall out of your vagina under its own weight. If it does not, you can help it out by bearing down during the contractions.

The best thing you can do to facilitate the third stage is to pick up your baby immediately after it is born, holding it close to your body while staying up. Putting your baby to the breast, or just having skin contact, encourages the release of oxytocin, which in turn stimulates the contraction of the uterus and helps in the separation and expulsion of the placenta.

When the cord stops pulsating, it is time for it to be clamped and cut.

'She fed, or rather nestled, and found comfort in my warm body. No syntometrine – there was no time to even think about it; the placenta was delivered seven minutes after the baby. There were no complications.'

'I put him to the breast and gazed at him while we waited for the placenta to be delivered. It took approximately forty minutes and then we were able to cut the cord. Although the midwives felt it was a long time to wait, we hardly noticed. It seemed more like five minutes.'

Once the placenta is expelled, the uterus is able to contract even further, and the cervix closes. During labour, your uterus has reversed – in a matter of hours – the process of its growth during the nine months of pregnancy, returning to its original orientation within your body and almost to its original size.

The process of birth is now complete and your baby begins his life as a separate person.

> 'I saw his little squashed face and enormous testicles, and knew he was mine. The feeling as he lay spluttering and slippering against my breast, with Nic's tearful face above him, is something I will never forget. I clumsily put him to my nipple and he opened one eye and looked quizzically up at us . . . The sense of achievement after the birth was enormous and best described by the first thing I said to Nic as we gazed adoringly at our son: "We did it!"'

Karoline's Story: Karoline Feuerbach's account of the births of her two daughters

Karoline's first labour lasted thirty hours – she missed two nights' sleep – and was very painful. Perhaps she expected too much of the birth? She had certainly prepared very assiduously for it. The second one was shorter, although still painful; but what made the main difference was the greater degree of active, conscious control. Here the Alexander Technique really came into its own.

I prepared myself for the birth of my first child with Leboyer's singing and breathing techniques, yoga for pregnancy, reading, anatomical studies and more. As an Alexander teacher, the technique had become part of my everyday life anyway.

I was very excited about the first birth. I had been able to maintain a good strong back throughout the pregnancy. I continued to enjoy teaching and working on myself and having an occasional Alexander lesson for myself. Lying on my back on the floor to release and direct myself was no problem right up to the birth. I felt apprehensive but also confident.

The contractions started at 10 o'clock in the evening. I had spent the afternoon in town at the school were my husband was training to become an Alexander teacher; the morning had been spent decorating as we had just moved. We got home to our house in a ski resort in freshly fallen snow.

I was already pretty exhausted. We rang the midwife in town who listened to my contractions over the phone and said to ring back in the morning. I was excited and wide awake. We cleaned the house and prepared the room for the birth. I was singing away *à la* Leboyer. Lying down was impossible, as the pain was too strong in that position; and I preferred to walk. This way I sat and walked all night. When the midwife came and left again after breakfast the next morning, asking to be rung later, I was pretty disappointed and a bit discouraged. She had just advised me to stop singing during contractions to prevent myself from getting hoarse before the real labour started. The 'real labour'? I felt I was labouring intensely already and impatience was setting in as well as utter fatigue.

I went on through the day and the midwife returned in the late afternoon. After examining me again, she didn't announce the birth as imminent but told me to be prepared for another night. At that point I was losing consciousness between contractions. I had been crying with exhaustion and pain and I felt at the end of my tether. The Alexander Technique? I was too tired, too exhausted to think about it. I was also despairing. I would have done anything to get out of the whole situation.

As it happened, the ski resort was in a village high up in the mountains a long drive away from the hospital. I wanted a home birth and dreaded hospitals. At the moment when the midwife told me that she did not know what to do any more and would phone the hospital I got very angry. I could not imagine forty minutes in the back of the car coping with contractions and driving down endless curves on icy roads. I also could not imagine being in a hospital at that point. I was angry with the midwife, angry with Leboyer, angry with my yoga teacher (who in my eyes had been glorifying the whole 'birth business'), angry with myself and everything around me. In this way the final contraction started. My anger had got me in touch with my strength again. If anyone had mentioned the Alexander Technique at that point or asked me to free my neck, I probably would have hit them. I was in pain and unconscious of anything else. My baby was born shortly afterwards. My only thought was that this was more pain than anyone could bear. I was not even angry any more.

As soon as the birth was over I felt wonderful, elated, full of energy. A healthy baby in my arms, there had been no complications, I had not even torn. The midwife put 'a gentle birth' on the papers. I thought this was a joke at the time and only later knew what she meant. I went into the shower, the midwife changed the sheets, we went back to bed cuddling and cooing. It was almost breakfast time. There followed the two happiest days of my life.

When I found myself pregnant again, I felt a strong aversion to all techniques advertising a 'gentle birth'. I had long talks with the midwife and a doctor and I went to a maternity hospital to find out about all ways of giving birth, including the conventional ones. I looked at the possibilities of taking painkillers and I looked at what it meant to have a Caesarean birth. When I had also informed myself about the effect conventional techniques can have on the child to be born, I understood the term 'gentle birth'. It meant gentle for the child and not – as I had imagined – also gentle for me.

I decided to have my baby at home again, and again use no painkillers. But I allowed myself the possibility of going down to hospital at any time during the labour if I wanted to. I was preparing myself differently this time. I also prepared my husband differently. He had been there the first time and had been a great moral support. This time I asked him to always remind me of the Alexander Technique directions: to keep my neck free, to let my head go forward and up, to let my back lengthen and widen. The midwife told us after the birth that she often had husbands who made a nuisance of themselves trying to help. She admitted that when she first heard these instructions, she thought this sort of support work very odd! She was later amazed at its effectiveness and really admired our teamwork. (She is now taking Alexander lessons herself!)

I had hoped to be able to keep in touch with my neck-head-back relationship (the 'primary control') at least during the intervals between contractions and in this way conserve my energy better. I also wanted to keep the directions going during a contraction – if that was possible.

Contractions started at 4 o'clock in the morning. I stayed in bed and listened to my body and felt better prepared this time. I could observe what the contractions were doing to me. I found I was able to consciously release the tension that would creep in as the pain increased. I could feel myself tensing up my pelvis, slightly holding my breath and tightening neck and shoulders. I then talked to my pelvis, telling it to release and soften, visualizing it widening and opening, telling my breathing to continue normally and my neck and shoulders to be free. This I experienced as looking at the pain without emotion rather than turning away from it. I visualized the baby being pushed down and the cervix being opened with each contraction. I also imagined that the pain was caused by the opening and that I wanted the opening to happen. This helped to make the pain much more bearable.

I found it did not matter too much which position I was in, as long as I was aware enough to give myself directions. If I could first of all direct my neck to be free, the rest of the directions to release would arrive faster; and would be supported by the key parts of my body already being less tense. I also made sure to send these directing thoughts during the intervals rather than collapse in a heap, which was more what I felt like doing. In this way I made myself conscious at all times and lessened the contrast between the high activity of contractions and the low activity of the intervals between them.

A contraction felt like an enormous involuntary muscle tension, which caused me to tense up many parts of my body that had nothing to do with the contraction itself. With the Alexander Technique, I would release this extra tension that was not needed and thus save much energy. When I did not collapse during the intervals, I felt more alert and less 'unprepared' as the next contraction started. To keep the right muscle tone during a period of rest also meant feeling more in control and not losing my energy completely. I could also look at the next moment and decide what to do: to change my position, drink some tea or just rest and enjoy the feeling of muscle release, which came close to blissfulness at times.

I felt much less a victim of the situation this time. Three times during this phase I experienced something like a miracle. The first time I had a contraction, it lasted for about fifteen minutes, and I almost fainted with pain. I went to bed afterwards, announcing that I was too exhausted to go on. But I gave myself directions and I noticed that I was not in a panic about not being able to continue, nor did I feel I was giving up. The midwife was wonderful. She told me to rest or even sleep if I could and this took the last bit of my fear of not being able to cope with the next contraction if it came. I closed my eyes and rested for an hour. I had dilated 7 cm by that time, being over half way through the birth. Miraculously, when I felt that I could cope again, contractions re-started and I got up.

This happened twice more with shorter periods of rest. Each time I felt incredibly grateful and very much at peace with the whole process. I knew that because I was not fighting, but was instead very much working consciously with the directions, my body was able to find its own speed and rhythm.

I had not been able to allow this to happen during the first birth. The pain seemed to be just as strong during the second birth but I was able to handle it very differently. I was keeping in touch with my body; I dared to listen. I needed no reminding from my husband to 'keep my neck free' until the final contractions.

When this phase started, I found myself searching for a position. During both pregnancies I had found a low crouching position very comfortable, but I could not use this position now. During the final stage of the first birth I had been on all fours. This time I found myself lying half reclining on my side, with my husband supporting my back. It seemed the oddest position, holding one knee with my hand; but it worked.

Now my husband came in with his reminders to keep my neck free. I experienced these final contractions as if I wanted to arch my whole back, beginning by tightening my neck and pulling my head back and down into my shoulders. When my husband told me to free my neck, he could not 'do' that for me, I had to send these thoughts myself. When they took effect, I experienced a softening, almost a rounding of my back, instead of the hard arching. I could then feel the head of the baby moving through the birth canal. This was an amazing experience which I did not have during the first birth. My wrong reaction to the pain had blocked out my ability to be aware of anything.

This time I was actually enjoying the birth. I had thought this was only possible for those 'other women' who were lucky enough to be 'better', 'more in touch with their bodies', or 'more natural'. The midwife helped me greatly by touching the baby's head and the point of the birth canal that it had got to. This reminded me to stay with the process, as the pain of the contractions made me want to put my awareness somewhere else every time.

This way my second baby was born. It had been a very conscious process and I felt enriched by the experience. This time I felt I had taken a big hurdle gracefully thanks to the Technique. I felt I was able to cope with an enormous amount of stress confidently. The second birth did not leave me in a state of elation afterwards as the first one had done. We never got around to lighting a candle during the birth or making the room look pretty or burning the lamp with the lavender and rose oil as we had done during the first birth. I stayed in my old working trousers till the final contractions started, the babysitter was preparing lunch outside and life seemed to go on as usual. I did not expect it to be a wonderful or even 'spiritual' experience; and as it turned out I was elated by the way I had handled the pain rather than by it being all over.

In writing about my experience of the birth, I have put a lot of emphasis on dealing with pain. Somehow this was an element I had missed in all the preparation work I had done for the first birth. The techniques had talked about the 'gentle way of giving birth' and I felt angry afterwards about not being better prepared for the 'painfulness of giving birth'. I do see the point of looking at the positive side and I also see the danger of increasing the fear of giving birth. I was very scared before the second birth and yet this made me deal with the pain better.

Once you know how to free your neck and how to keep it free, it is a matter of remembering to do so and even wanting to do so. Faced with a contraction, my 'natural' reaction was to tense up and dread the prospect of pain. My body just tensed in the hope of preventing the pain from being overwhelming. Freeing the neck was like admitting the pain. Freeing the neck meant being very honest, not shying away from what there was to come. It also meant allowing to happen what should happen and not preventing it. When contractions came, it meant allowing them to open the cervix. This way I could feel what the contraction was doing, that it was opening me, opening the way for my baby. It seemed that this way each contraction was doing its job properly and I was not getting in its way.

The Alexander Technique is not a technique somebody can do for you. It is not like massage or acupressure which leaves you passive and receptive. Having a husband who is an Alexander Teacher obviously helped me – but even he could not 'do' the freeing of the neck or deal with any other tension for me. You can learn how to send these directions or thoughts into your body, causing an 'undoing of tension'; and then apply this learning during birth. If you can do this, the Alexander Technique can work wonders!

Karoline Feuerbach
Germany
November 1992

5

You and Your Baby

What is it going to be like when your baby is born? Some first-time parents don't give much thought to what will happen after the birth. It may be seen as the *end* of story, like the 'happy ever after' of a fairy tale. But when a baby is born – particularly your first – it is the beginning of a whole new way of life.

You may feel quite euphoric and have boundless energy to carry you through the first few days and nights. Alternatively, it may have been a really difficult birth, perhaps a Caesarean section, and many women experience the so-called 'baby blues', sapping even the will to cope. It can be the most exhausting time of your life. If you have more than one youngster, you will need to deal with the demands on your time and energy from other family members, as well as the sheer volume of work a baby creates. How can the Alexander Technique help you in these early days and months?

Starting lessons soon after having had your baby is possible. Most women though, will find themselves too preoccupied in the first few weeks unless they have considerable practical assistance. It is more realistic, at this stage, to rely on a previously acquired knowledge and understanding of the Technique.

Although your baby will be your first priority, your ability to sustain your energy as a mother will depend a lot on you: women often assume responsibility for meeting every one else's needs before even stopping to consider their own; it is quite a challenge to stay in the 'here and now' and to take into account your own needs, as well as those of others. So, we shall focus on your process of recovery from the pregnancy and birth, before going on to discuss aspects of your baby's development: should you, as is often suggested, attempt to speed it up?

Looking After Yourself

'I had back problems after my first baby, caused by overdoing a stretching exercise, a few months after the birth. My second child has been so much more demanding than the first – a bad sleeper and later a problem teether; we've had some terrible nights! The Alexander lessons I'd had helped me cope so much better this time and, amazingly, I've had no back problems. Lying down in the Alexander way has been my main support and knowing how to bend well has been enormously helpful with all the lifting and carrying.'

Postnatal recovery

The obvious change in your body after the birth is the 'emptiness' within: the absence of the weight of your baby, the placenta and the fluid that surrounded it while it was in your womb. Over the next few days you will lose more weight as extra fluid contained in tissues is shed and blood volume returns to normal.

Good body use will greatly aid your process of recovery. Your uterus should return to its normal size within six weeks. Abdominal muscles that have stretched considerably to accommodate the baby will be quite slack at first, but should tone up again without the need to do special exercises. Your ligaments will continue to be soft for a few months and heavy lifting and over-stretching should be avoided. Even if you didn't tear or have an episiotomy, your perineum will feel sore and tender after the birth. As exhaustion catches up and you feed your baby round the clock, it is very easy to pull down into yourself. The Alexander Technique can help you maintain a more expanded posture and cope better with lack of sleep.

Your need for rest

With your body sense registering more accurately, you will know whether you are making too much effort, wasting energy needlessly. The drive to 'end-gain' – 'I must get such and such done before making supper' – will be seen for what it is: self-destructive, if not checked. Resist the temptation to catch up on all the chores whenever your baby sleeps. Use some of that time for recuperation, keeping something in reserve, particularly if you have other young children to take care of. You will be more able to accommodate any sudden demands that may crop up.

Your daily routine before the birth, of lying down and releasing tension through giving directions, may seem impossible to reinstate with the constant demands made on your time now, but will help you re-charge your batteries and facilitate any healing which may be needed. Now you will have to fit your rest times around your baby's needs.

In the first few weeks, give yourself a good half an hour to lie down in the middle of the day as described on pp. 45–51, with your head supported and your legs bent. You may want to extend your arms to the sides (the 'crucifix' position, the elbows slightly bent) to to form a 'W' with your arms to the sides and beyond your head, to help undo any pulling down from feeding or carrying your baby. It is more beneficial if you lie on a softly carpeted floor, than take to bed. You can always put your legs up on a bed or place a pillow – lengthways – or large cushion under each thigh, allowing the legs to roll gently outwards and the knees to soften. (In cold weather, cover yourself with a blanket for the last part of your quiet time so that, if you drift off to sleep, you will keep warm.) You may be able to persuade a toddler to have a sleep at the same time or an older child to play near you – although they probably won't let you sleep! And remember that the odd five or ten minutes rest, as needed during the day, can help you keep going.

The main resting position is on your back. Sometimes you may feel inclined to lie prone to ease yourself out. In this case you will need to put pillows under your hips and shoulders to prevent your back hollowing and your breasts becoming uncomfortable (although if they are very full you may find this never works); and your head should be turned to the side. This is supposed to be an excellent position for encouraging the pelvic organs to return to their proper relationship to each other. There is no reason, however, for thinking that it is any better than the semi-supine position or, more importantly, than using your body as well as you can during your daily activities.

After a Caesarean

While you are in bed recovering from the operation, the usual advice is to flex, extend and circle your feet from time to time to keep the muscle pumps in the leg veins working, and to prevent the risk of thrombosis. While doing this – and at other times as you think of it – renew your directions so that you do not lose too much general muscle tone in the short time you are confined to bed. If you had a general anaesthetic, you will need to cough to clear your chest. Let your abdominal muscles tighten (they should do so naturally on breathing out) when you cough, making a 'huffing' sound 'forwards and *out*' rather than 'forwards and *down*'. In general the Technique will help you to avoid pulling down into the discomfort, maintaining as much 'up' as possible.

Positioning yourself for feeding your baby

The Alexander Technique is concerned not so much with *position* as with *coordination* and *body use*. Nevertheless, you will find it useful to think about how you can minimize downward pressures on your spine – and the rest of the body – while you are feeding your baby.

Old-fashioned nursing chairs used to have flat, long backs and short legs (if you have not got such a chair, you can probably find something suitable and saw a little off the legs). Alternatively, you may find it more comfortable to sit on a firm sofa or bed surrounded by strategically placed cushions or pillows to help support you and your baby effectively. The aim should be to maintain an expanded posture and to have *your*

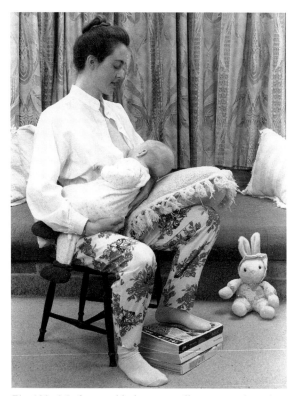

Fig. 133 Mother and baby are well supported, and the mother is able to maintain a lengthening and widening back.

baby raised to your breast if you are breastfeeding, rather than slumping and twisting your back to get your breast to the baby.

Positioning your baby   Your baby will be more comfortable, and will feed more effectively, if he is positioned well. Two good positions are, first, 'belly to belly' – your baby's belly against yours; and second, the baby placed to your side, his legs pointing backwards (this is especially useful after a Caesarean, avoiding pressure on the scar). In both of these, the baby's head needs to be supported in line with his spine, facing the breast, rather than having to turn his head to feed. Remember to place your nipple deep into the baby's mouth so that he sucks on as much of the areola as possible; you will run less risk of developing sore or cracked nipples, or blocked milk ducts.

Feeding without tension   Keep your body weight balanced evenly over your sitting bones, which should be positioned as close as possible to the back of your support. Place a bulky cushion behind you to help support your back comfortably, from the top of your pelvis to between your shoulder blades; lengthen and broaden against it, rather than slumping down away from – or into – it (a little of your weight will, of course, be on your feet). It can be a good idea to rest one foot on a small stool at the side on which you are feeding (a small cushion under your raised knee may be comfortable), and to raise your baby on a cushion or two (Fig. 133).

Be aware that your head balances on top of your neck approximately at the level of the middle of your ears. Allow your neck to release to let your head tilt gently forward so that you can look at your baby (without needing to poke your neck forward), while lengthening and broadening your back. Also give particular attention to your shoulders, allowing them to release and spread sideways; and let the extension continue down to the elbows. It is very easy to get into the bad habit of raising your shoulders when feeding; and you are more likely to be tense if you have sore or cracked nipples or a baby who frets at the breast. This is a good opportunity – as well as enjoying your baby – to revitalize yourself through energizing directions. (While your baby is no more than a few months old, you may be able to catch up on some reading, raising your book on a cushion or two on the other side.)

In bed, a firm pillow or piece of foam against the top of your pelvis and back can help prevent the pelvis tilting back and the lower back rounding excessively. A water-bed may be wonderful in other circumstances but it is not the place to nurse a baby; one young woman who came for lessons had seriously damaged two lumbar discs from 'sitting' on her lower back on a water-bed. You may find you can feed with ease lying on your side in bed, but, for some, it may restrict a part of the breast, causing the milk ducts to block and increasing the risk of mastitis.

Dealing with mastitis ('milk fever')

This can be a wretched and debilitating experience. It can occur as early as the first few days, before the milk supply is fully established. For some it may be a recurrent problem, not helped by a baby's erratic feeding, and even the tiniest untoward pressure on a breast may be enough to trigger another attack.

If the milk ducts are not cleared regularly, milk can stagnate, leading to inflammation and then infection. Make sure that your baby is feeding evenly from each breast and, if necessary, express a little milk – but there is a delicate balance between supply and demand especially in the early days. When your milk supply is more stable, expressing some milk may be the best solution. Positioning your baby well, as suggested – perhaps at your side – can help drain the affected breast more easily. Alternate hot and cold bathing to the affected breast and gentle massage – from the under-arm area towards the nipple, working all the way round – can provide local relief.

What else can you do to alleviate the problem? Stress can be a major factor, so releasing tension in your back and chest is very important, especially when feeding, to facilitate the blood and nerve supply to the breasts, and the lymphatic drainage. Try to avoid pulling down with the

Fig. 134

Fig. 135

Fig. 136

Fig. 137

Arm circling to help release middle back while maintaining the neck-head-back relationship.

weight of your breasts; a well-fitting, supportive bra is essential (although sometimes any restriction can aggravate the situation) as there are, of course, no muscles in breast tissue.

You may find crawling helpful, as described on pp. 66–70. Try, also, the following movement:

Circling the arms Practised from time to time, this T'ai Chi-based movement may assist in keeping the middle back free and improve breast function. It is also helpful for anyone who spends a lot of time sitting at a desk. *Note:* It requires an understanding of monkey and the use of the arms that we discussed on pp. 37–8. It is complex to describe it properly as with other movements suggested in the pregnancy and birth chapters – but refer to the pictures and put the instructions on to an audiotape if you wish, so that you can talk yourself through the movement until you have got the idea (Figs 134–137).

Begin with your feet turned slightly out, shoulder-width apart, and your knees slightly bent. Raise, say, your right arm to the side at shoulder level, the arm lengthening out but the elbow and wrist bent (like a bird's wing), shifting your weight onto your right leg, and keeping the length in your back; raise your left hand to shoulder level a foot or so in front of your upper chest (again elbow and wrist bent). Renew your directions to the primary control and let your shoulders release and spread sideways.

Bending your legs, circle your arms clockwise, down and across to the left, transferring your weight to your left leg, the left arm swinging gently across and up to the left, the right arm following and rising in front of your upper chest as your legs begin straightening.

While your legs straighten further (although they should not lock), your hands continue their gentle swinging movement up in front of your head as your weight moves to the right. Your right leg then bends, your right arm going out to the side (joints still bent) and your left hand comes in front of your upper chest. You are now passing through an earlier part of the movement and, as before, shift your weight across to the left, your arms circling down and across to the left and then up to shoulder level. Complete the first cycle of the movement with your left arm to the side, your right hand a foot or so in front of your chest, the legs having straightened a little. Pause and re-direct; you are now in the same position that you began this movement – but on the other side.

To repeat the movement – *but circling your arms in a counter-clockwise direction* – begin by letting the arms sweep down as the left leg bends once more and then shift to the right, and so on.

You should soon get the feeling for the rhythm of the movement if you don't rush it – the arm movements are given impetus by the shifting weight and the rising up out of a bend. The shoulders hardly need to lift. *It is essential to keep your neck and lower back released throughout this movement; and your spine should not twist or incline as the weight transfers to one side* (your teacher can help you perform the movement well). You should feel a gentle stretch between the shoulder blades and, monitoring the freedom of your neck – depending on the mobility of your shoulders – you can gradually extend the height at which the arms circle up as they rise above shoulder level.

Lifting and carrying your baby

To a parent, lifting and carrying young children seems never-ending. When they are very young they like to be carried much of the time; when older they are heavier and, if you have more than one, they'll all want to come on board at the same time!

The Alexander Technique can help you to recover muscle tone in a more efficient and balanced way, to avoid putting undue strain on ligaments that are still soft. First, we shall remind you of the dynamics of lifting and then the best ways of carrying your baby will be described.

Bending and lifting You will find the monkey and lunge, two basic ways of bending that have been discussed in detail on pp. 34–7, invaluable. In the early days, the full squat may be too uncomfortable, particularly if you have had stitches. Later on, if you can't squat comfortably with both heels down, an intermediate way of bending – first lunging and then using the monkey, letting the back heel lift off the floor as you bend – can be especially useful. It gives you good stability – and the possibility of shifting your weight while bending.

Lifting from the floor presents no special problems. The basic principle is always to remind yourself: stop before lifting; release your neck and shoulders and think of your head lifting out of the top of your neck in opposition to your feet, which drive down, your spine lengthening and your legs engaging in the lift last of all (see Figs. 138–140).

Lifting your baby in and out of a cot, play-pen or car can, however, be very taxing. You will need to minimize the tendency to make top-heavy movements and to use the back as a crane (there are no hinge joints in the back). To bend over a cot and play-pen, the basic movement is to combine lunge with monkey; with a cot it is usually possible to lower one side, enabling you to bend lower and closer to your baby (Fig. 141).

Moving a heavier child in or out of a car seat in cramped conditions is a real hazard for the back. Try to get your front leg as far forward as possible to reduce the forward bending, especially if you have to lean over to the other side of the car (this can be avoided if you get inside the car); ideally your foot is placed forward, but often your knee will be used to support the weight. You will have to do the best you can in a situation which is not ideal, trying to maintain as much freedom and expansion as possible and avoiding jerky movements. So long as you don't twist your spine while lifting, the occasional movement which is not perfect should not be a problem for a back that is being used well most of the time.

Fig. 138

Fig. 139

Fig. 140

Fig. 141   Awkward lifting is made easier by the use of lunge and monkey.

Figs 138–140   The head releases out of a free neck, the spine lengthens and the legs engage last of all.

Bathing baby and changing nappies (diapers)   You may find yourself needing to kneel when bathing your baby in the family bath (the panel being in the way) or when using a bath on a stand, or changing a nappy on the floor; but in these situations you can place one foot to the side and a little forward. This gives you more room for manoeuvre and makes it easier to avoid arching the back. When changing a nappy, you may prefer to do so at a moderately raised surface such as a bed or sofa, because it is easier on your back (Fig. 142). If you use a changing table, beware of locking your knees and pulling down. Finally, when you make asymmetric movements such as the lunge, or kneeling on one leg, try to vary the side on which you do most of the work.

Carrying   Avoid 'mother's hip' (it affects fathers as well!): the habit of carrying the baby supported on one hip that juts out to the side, is very harmful. The lower spine takes the brunt of the downward pressure and twisting forces, and the intervertebral discs become more vulnerable to shearing forces and damage; sacro-iliac (where the sacrum – the base of the spine – joins with the pelvis) strain can also be caused (Fig. 143).

Instead, carry your baby closer to your centre of gravity. This means that your arm(s) and shoulder(s) do a little more work, but if you remember to let your weight move a little forward of your heels, keeping your knees soft and letting your lengthening and broadening back do the bulk of the work, your body will be under less strain (Fig. 144). If you are standing for some time, try placing one foot a half-step in front of the other, join your fingers together to create a 'sling' and use the arm (on the same side as the forward foot) to crook your baby, resting the forearm on your front hip and remembering to broaden across your back and shoulders.

Slings and carriers   To carry your baby for any length of time, a well-designed 'sling' can be very useful. It is very comforting for your baby to be held close to you and to be in movement with you; and it can make shopping a tolerable social experience for you both. Even then, it can be exhausting and quite a strain, so try not to overdo things. The sling will tend to pull you forward and down and most people will compensate by swaying back. To prevent this, keep renewing the lengthening directions to your spine while encouraging your lower back to widen.

For a child who is much older than six months, some kind of baby carrier on your back is better when using a push-chair or stroller is impracticable. Choose one that has adequately padded shoulder straps and a waist strap.

With your baby in the carrier on your back, the forces on you are not unlike those produced by carrying a rucksack, except that it will be more difficult: the baby's weight will be located higher up your back than the contents of a rucksack (as well as being more mobile). The shoulder straps will tend to pull your upper torso back, causing a sway-back, and

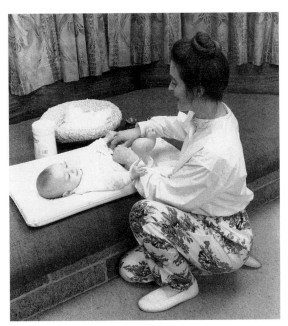

Fig. 142 Taking care to avoid pulling down while changing baby.

Fig. 143 'Mother's hip' can harm the lower back.

Fig. 144 Carrying the baby without swaying back.

the inclination will be to compensate by pushing your head and neck forward. *The secret is to lean slightly forward over your ankles, keeping your weight between the heels and balls of your feet; and while lengthening (and this is where the waist strap comes in) let your lower back 'swell out' backwards, keeping your knees slightly bent in opposition to the lower back so that the pelvis doesn't tilt forwards.* (Note: the body mechanics are similar to carrying your baby late in pregnancy.)

A final consideration is the baby's head support, whether as part of the sling or part of the carrier. By about four months, most babies will have developed some head control, but whether it's a child of this age, or a two-year-old, when they fall asleep – as they frequently do while being carried – the head will lurch, and so proper support is important. Even the better carriers currently available seem to need additional padding round the sides.

Push-chairs (strollers) and prams (baby carriages)   As well as choosing one that has firm, straight back support for your baby, ensure that the handle is at the right height for you: the ideal height is between hip level and your navel so that it is easier to push from your centre of gravity. If you and your partner are of different heights, it is worth looking out for a push-chair with an adjustable handle.

One of the sights that can make an Alexander teacher cringe with horror (although she will endeavour to keep her own neck free at the same time!) is a parent struggling up a hill with a push-chair: the handle is often too low and too far in front of over-extended arms; the parent is stooped, with head down and jammed back, lower back arched, pelvis tilted forward and buttocks sticking out, and the legs full of tension (Fig. 145). (You can probably think of plenty of other pushing movements that are made with unnecessary strain.)

Ask yourself where the push is coming from in your body: it should come from your centre of gravity. The movement required is to walk as we have described earlier, your legs remaining slightly more bent than on level ground; with your elbows dropped and your shoulders released, the push-chair – close to you – will 'get out of the way' as you advance (Fig. 146). Remember that your hands do not generally need to *grip* the handles or bar: they can rest lightly, fingers relaxed. When pushing uphill, use the heel, not the ball of the hands, again releasing tension in the fingers; when going downhill, allow the fingers to gently 'stay' the movement. With a double push-chair you will need to pay particular attention to your body use; if you have one where one child sits in front of the other, you will find it easier to place the heavier child closest to you.

Playing with your baby

You will be spending a lot of time not only attending to, but increasingly playing with your baby. This is so valuable, not only for baby and for your relationship with him, but also for you; you will learn a lot from

Fig. 145 'Top-heavy' pushing creates a lot of tension.

Fig. 146 Easy, powerful, well-coordinated pushing.

Fig. 147

being with him, observing him, doing things at his pace; and he will gain from the all-important interaction with you (Fig. 147).

To begin with, you will probably place him on a rug or blanket, allowing him to kick and gurgle and explore his hands, feet and toys. As your baby becomes more active, he will practise lifting his head, following you with his eyes and trying to turn himself over. Gradually he will become more proficient, rolling over, trying to sit and crawl or shuffle. At this stage, you lose some of your freedom and he will start to clamber onto you whenever he can. You can crawl with him, remembering to give directions, while you enjoy his emerging ease of movement.

There will be a lot of 'floor work' in the next few years, so it is worth finding good ways of moving and being at this level: for instance, sitting cross-legged or tailor fashion if you have enough flexibility in your hip and pelvic areas (otherwise sit on a cushion to raise your seat bones to make it easier). For long periods, place your sitting bones close to a wall or piece of furniture against which you can lengthen and widen your back. You may prefer to squat, or to sit or kneel with one foot forward alternating sides from time to time. If you are tired or uncomfortable, try lying down nearby in the semi-supine position.

It is best to avoid altogether sitting with your legs to one side, as this will put pressure on your lower back and twist it; and sitting on the ground between the legs – a collapsed kneeling position, which stresses the knees and back.

In the playground Playground activities involve pushing, lifting, carrying and bending. When you put your baby into a swing, remember to lift with care, not bending from the waist or arching the back. Pushing a swing has some parallels with 'driving' a push-chair except that you let go! You will use the lunge; remember where the push should come from, and let yourself find a gentle, easy rhythm, shifting your weight forwards and backwards (notice how most people tense up in this activity). Squatting in sand – whether in the playground or on the beach – can be easier than on the flat and is a good place (while building sand-castles) to develop more suppleness.

Getting back into 'shape'?

What shape should your body be? What has been fashionable in the 80s – a 'tight' body – may be changing to one that is more rounded. Ought you to sacrifice yourself to passing trends? Why can't we be who we are? – part of which is using our bodies well, as nature intended. Many women feel driven to diet after the birth: they want to get their weight down quickly to what it used to be. However, there is evidence that dieting has unintended consequences: the metabolic rate drops so that calories are more efficiently absorbed; and when normal quantities of food are eaten again, or when bingeing occurs in reaction to previous self-denial, weight goes on more easily than before. Add to this obsessive exercising, and we have a whole syndrome of denial and over-control.

This, of course, is all 'end-gaining'; perhaps we would be better off finding a more balanced way of eating, where changes in weight can take place spontaneously and gradually, as we tune in to our body's signals – and gain more insight into our emotional needs.

Do I need to do special exercises   You have probably heard that unless you do certain exercises, you won't 'get your figure back'. Is this true? And is it a feasible goal anyway? Carrying your baby over all those months and giving birth means that your body has changed: whether you breastfeed or not, your breasts won't recover their pre-pregnancy shape; and stretch marks, if you have them, may fade but won't go away completely. Your body has opened out to let a new life grow inside it, and it has had to open up further to let that new life emerge into the world. And after a first baby you are physiologically more 'primed', as a general rule, for easier subsequent births.

Once the enormous demands of the first few months are over, many women feel light and energized and, if they do not fear another pregnancy, may experience an increase in their sexual drive and satisfaction. This tendency to a greater openness is naturally reflected in the muscle tone of the body. And so, without being flabby, the musculature – which has now been more stretched and exercised – will have a somewhat different quality. The goal of trying to acquire a 'tight' body, including the emphasis on a flat tummy (as discussed earlier), is very questionable. To have your figure back *exactly* as it was before is impossible and, if attempted, will almost certainly lead to undesirable tension, as well as frustration when you don't succeed. Most of the toning exercises recommended postnatally involve contracting the abdominal muscles and the buttocks in order, it is claimed, to maintain a 'correct' pelvic tilt. They are best avoided: inevitably, they bring about tension in other parts of the body, producing a generalized pulling down, and they impair free movement; restriction and pressure in the abdominal and pelvic areas will interfere with normal functioning in the organs disturbed by this muscular strait-jacket. *Good body use in daily life - particularly in bending movements like the monkey, lunge and squat – will gradually, effectively and naturally restore tone in slack muscles. This is essentially all that is required.* When your baby is a few weeks old, you might want to have some more lessons. Your baby can, of course, go with you; he may sleep, or your teacher can work with you while you are doing whatever is necessary!

The only special exercises you will probably need to do will be the pelvic floor exercises described on p. 82, remembering of course to give attention to your primary control. They can be done in bed in the first days after the birth, in the 'semi-supine' position. You can also practise 'whispered ahs' (see pp. 52–3), giving directions to lengthen your back, and this will gently help tone the whole abdominal area (while avoiding tightness of the jaw and throat).

Later, as your baby becomes less dependent on you, you will probably feel the need to take more exercise. We have already mentioned some forms of exercise: long walks, swimming, Medau and perhaps most of all for the range and aesthetic of the movement, T'ai Chi – all these can be beneficial if carried out with attention to using your body well. T'ai Chi is of special value in that a wide range of flowing and gently toning movements – calming yet energizing – are performed slowly, developing mind-body awareness and recovering much of the suppleness of the young child.

Your Baby's Development

There is much to see and marvel at in the extraordinary process of children's development. How is it that infants have such a capacity to acquire, spontaneously, all the basic psycho-physical skills?

Stages of development

Let's consider, briefly, the early stages of the baby's control of his own body. Head control comes first, in the early months, and is necessary before the child can sit unsupported. Most babies will crawl before standing and walking, although some will move sideways, crab-like, or shuffle along on their buttocks.

Just before walking, infants are able to bend their legs, supporting, raising and lowering the body with ease – soon, to a full squat. It is a strikingly beautiful movement to see (Fig. 148) and so different from the

Fig. 148   An eight-month-old infant shows all the features of
bending most of us need to recover later.

top-heavy bending that becomes habitual later.

Within it are the basic elements of coordination that, unfortunately, most of us need to re-learn in later years: the free neck – remarkable considering the proportionately large head; the way the head initiates and leads movement so that in rising from full squat to standing there is no strain. Compare that with the way most of us bend and lift, especially if we try to do the movement 'correctly'. To avoid back strain we are told to bend the knees: it is not only a matter, though, of the knees flexing, but also the hips and ankles; and the work of the legs needs to be secondary to the neck-head-back relationship. We are also advised to keep the back straight while bending – but this tends to create stiffness in the back and neck, instead of the easy lengthening of the spine and the capacity to pivot forward, as required, from the hips.

Baby exercises?

Is it your duty as a parent – unless there are congenital problems – to make special efforts to accelerate your baby's coordination skills? One

Fig. 149 Coming out of a spiralling movement, the head leads. See the poised purposefulness of this infant.

exercise that is widely advocated illustrates just what is wrong with such an approach. To encourage your baby's head control – a pre-requisite for unsupported sitting – it is often suggested that you pull him up, from lying on his back, by his arms. This laboured sit-up, however, is quite different from the graceful means that an infant actually employs by himself to get up by a *spiralling* movement, rolling on to the side first (Fig. 149).

Since children learn so much by imitation, the parents' main priority should be to make modest attempts to improve their own coordination. Then, the physical handling – the holding, the hugging, the lifting and the carrying – will transmit less tension to the child. This will help maintain the exquisite sensitivity of his body sense.

Surely, it is preferable to enjoy playing with your baby in a safe and varied environment, where you are alert to him and responding to what he wants to do? If you allow him the space and the freedom to explore himself and the world – and trust the process – you can watch the stages of development, in the normal, healthy child, unfolding in front of you; he will not need special assistance. Children differ a great deal in their level of activity and in the rate and precise manner of their development. Little enough is known about this and it is, perhaps, presumptuous to try to improve on the wondrous intricacy of the normal infant's developing body-mind. (If you are at all worried that your baby's development is not what it should be, do seek professional advice.)

Bouncers, walkers and other equipment

Now we shall consider some of the baby equipment flooding the market. Before buying anything, ask yourself whether it does what it claims to do and whether it could have any undesirable effects: for example, will it be good for your child's body use?

A 'bouncing cradle' can be a great help in the first few months (though a very active baby may not tolerate the restriction), satisfying the baby's need both to be close to you and to be rocked, as well as your need to get basic things done. The main thing to look for – which is true of any kind of baby carrier – is that, rather than sagging like a deck-chair, support for the back should be firm and straight.

A 'bouncer' that hangs from a door-frame so that the baby can extend his legs, jumping up and down, may be useful when sufficient head control has developed. There are a number of provisos: some babies don't take to them at all, so try one before you buy; also it can be quite awkward getting the baby set up in it without dropping him, so take care!; and, finally, babies should not be left in these bouncers for too long – perhaps no more than twenty minutes – because an over-emphasis on strengthening the leg extensors may actually hinder their walking development.

A 'sit-in walker', where the baby does not have to balance himself, allows him to be more mobile than he otherwise would be and can be a great temptation for a busy parent. But the baby doesn't actually need this, so why not let him find his own mobility? 'Push-along walkers' on wheels allow a more natural progression of skills in standing and walking but can sometimes run away with the baby. These often work better on a thick pile carpet, grass or sand. Given time and the freedom to move, your baby will soon take care of his own walking, anyway.

So, as far as babies and toddlers are concerned, it's best to leave developing well alone. Unfortunately, children's body use starts to deteriorate towards the end of the pre-school years and declines further – alarmingly – through childhood and adolescence. Why this happens, and what might be done by parents and teachers – and children themselves – to prevent this, is the subject of the final chapter.

6

Our Children's Potential: Alexander's Insights

> The characteristic note of true happiness is struck when the healthy child is busily engaged in doing something which interests it.
>
> *FM Alexander*[1]

By the age of eighteen, many young people show signs of disturbance in their physical and mental functioning. Absence of marked postural defects – head and neck poked forward, hunched shoulders, tilted pelvis, sway-back, locked knees and so on – is the *exception* in this age group.[2] Recent surveys have found that as many as twenty-five per cent of adolescents experience back pain, and for some it lasts more than a week.[3] Children nowadays seem to have a shorter attention span, and disaffection with life is becoming a major problem: 'alienated, anxious and addicted to TV' and obsessed with their physical appearance, were the findings of a recent study of eleven to fourteen year olds in England.[4] And we have all heard statistics on the prevalence of back pain in adults.

What is going wrong? We live in an increasingly uncertain time where the role of education – itself undergoing tremendous upheaval in recent years – is being hotly debated. What should be the responsibility of teachers, and what can we do as parents?

One of Alexander's leading teacher trainers of his Technique, Patrick Macdonald, remarked that education is the name given to ·'processes whereby children are robbed of their natural inheritance', and that the work of Alexander teachers is one of re-education: 'We give them back some part of that of which they have been robbed.'[5] Alexander, however, had a vision of education informed by a deep understanding of the discoveries he had made. John Dewey (1859–1952) – perhaps the foremost American philosopher of the first half of this century – whose ideas have had a major influence on the development of educational practice today, wrote the introductions to three of Alexander's books. In the *Use of the Self* he states:

Without knowledge of what constitutes a truly normal and healthy psycho-physical life, our professed education is likely to be mis-education ... The technique of FM Alexander gives to the educator a standard of psycho-physical health ... It supplies also the 'means whereby' this standard may be progressively and endlessly achieved, becoming a conscious possession of the one educated. It provides, therefore, the conditions for the central direction of all special educational processes. *It bears the same relation to education that education bears to all other activities.*[6] [our italics]

This is an enormous claim for Dewey to make (it is quite clear that he was fully aware of its implications) – and it is one that we shall also argue. Are we any closer to the kind of education we want for our children? If teachers, parents and children had some understanding of the Alexander Technique, what would that mean for children's learning?

First, we shall identify some of the causes of the misuse that affects most of us by adult life. Children's development will then be traced through infancy, young childhood and adolescence. What insights do Alexander's 'operational' ideas, discussed in Chapter 1, generate? At each stage we shall examine what you might do as parent or teacher to prevent misuse, and its associated problems, arising; and we shall also look at what youngsters can do for themselves.

How We Go Wrong

Very young children are extremely sensitive, 'open' and impressionable, acting as 'emotional barometers' of their families' stresses and strains. They show no obvious division of the mental and physical, expressing their feelings and frustrations intensely, immediately, and physically. But a kind of 'deadening' – a loss of expansiveness, of energy, of enthusiasm – seems to set in, sometimes from an early age. By adolescence they may be surly, sullen and 'cut off' not only from others, but from a large part of themselves. Parents can be so pre-occupied with 'getting by' that they do not really listen to, or respect, their children's interests and concerns.

There are many factors that gradually erode the confidence, ease of movement and poise of the pre-school child. Perhaps the most important is imitation – largely unconscious – of those around him: his parents, initially, then teachers and other children (peer pressure is incredibly strong: children are commonly ridiculed for appearing 'different'); and, later on, the role models of youth culture. In doing so, he begins to take on the poor use and tension habits of those with whom he has contact or identifies.

As he gets older, school exerts a greater influence. School and home can be a partnership but some parents hand over much of the responsibility for their children's learning to schools, failing to see the value of their own contribution. At school, the general atmosphere and approach to learning will have a profound effect on the child's 'use of the self'. We must never forget that he is *required* to be there. This can be a very negative experience and he is likely to feel out of control of his own learning much of the time, which can create feelings of anxiety, boredom and confusion and the seeds of failure.[7]

Teachers are increasingly struggling in 'survival mode' in the classroom, and the child's individual needs will inevitably be subordinated to the system's requirement of handling large classes. Emotional stresses may come to weigh more heavily on him, affecting his body image and the way he holds himself. He will also be sitting for longer than is desirable at furniture that is not the proper size for him: the older children at primary school often grow out of its furniture some time before they move on to secondary school. At an increasingly early age, he will be expected to use computers; the question of how he *uses himself* while manipulating the machine is unlikely to be addressed at all. The physical activities he will engage in – the gymnastics, the dance, the sports and games – do not adequately compensate for the imbalances created for having to sit too long in awkward positions, and may even make things worse: he will bring the same deteriorating body sense to all his activities; and changes in alignment from accidents and injuries sustained earlier may have become habitual.

We may not see the effects of all these influences on our children's use: they are insidious and commonplace, and we take them for granted (looking back, it is hard to say when deterioration set in). And children won't complain if they are not taken seriously – they get used to conforming to our expectations. Human beings have great capacity to live with distortions, whether physical or emotional (and usually both); by the time functioning is impaired, grave deterioration in 'the use of the self' is usually firmly established.

The pre-school child

The pre-school child learns at a phenomenal rate. A child's brain at one year is two-thirds of its adult weight; by two years the structure of the cortex is essentially no different from that of the adult brain – most of the main interconnections of nerve fibres have been made; and by five years, the brain is 90% of its mature weight.[8]

Muscles develop from the head down and from the centre of the body to the peripheries. The earliest sign of controlled muscle movement – compared with reflex activity – is the control of neck muscles: by six to eight months, most infants are well on the way to being able to sit unsupported (Fig. 150). While bones increase in size and weight throughout childhood, it is not generally appreciated that some bones are not present at birth: for instance, by twelve months three wrist bones will have appeared and the other six are formed during childhood and adolescence. Nerve pathways to the thumb and index finger do not mature until five to seven years old (in girls generally earlier than in boys). These facts of physical development have enormous implications for the development of manual skills and are why the development of

Fig. 150   The head 'supports' the whole body in a beautifully balanced way.

the fine control needed for handwriting skills takes time.

Toddlers are usually pot-bellied and sway-backed because tummy and back muscles are not so well developed, the liver is larger and the bladder is not yet in the pelvic cavity. Walking occurs at about one year. By two years or so, the child is not so top-heavy, walks on a narrower base and begins to lean slightly forward when walking, the ankles flexing so that the heels go down just in advance of the rest of the feet. Walking with longer steps and then running emerges at this time. By three years of age, he is able to balance on one leg for a few seconds (most adults can't do this easily); and he is experimenting with holding a pencil more like an adult instead of gripping it with all his fingers. Muscle size increases rapidly in proportion to body weight; this is a time of great and often restless action as increasingly sustained and skilled activities are undertaken. The more the child can do, and the more he has opportunities to practise his skills – as he chooses to – the more they will develop (Figs. 151–153).

As far as psychological growth is concerned, most children appear to have a strong sense of self by eighteen months to two years old; for example they can clearly recognize themselves in mirrors or photographs (the beginnings of body images – of size and shape – comes six months later). Bladder and bowel control begin to be exercised. At this time of explosive language development, one of the words most often uttered is 'no!'.

The Alexander Technique

Alexander occasionally worked with children as young as two years old. The overall experience in the Alexander world of working in the usual lesson format with pre-school children is very limited – and almost certainly not the most effective way of meeting their needs. So what is the relevance of the Technique to the pre-school child?

Much will be conveyed indirectly through the parent's state of mind-body. We do not know how big a part of the consciousness of children at this age is made up of sensory information, but we do know that in later years thoughts and emotional preoccupations can block out much of our body awareness. The parents' presence, tone of voice, the 'listening' quality of their touch, all have their immediate effects on their children. Again, the onus is on us to reflect on our influence on them: we don't have to be perfect – that's not how life is! – but we can allow the possibility of change as we feel able to.

An important part of a child's sense of self is self-esteem. Telling and showing our children that we love them, especially when we have just been angry with them, is very important. A useful working premise in our dealings with children – which will foster their independence and self-confidence – is that they are just like adults, but short on experience and the knowledge which derives from that. Unless the child is doing something which is dangerous, it may be preferable to intervene only when asked to. Our urge to interfere may reflect our drive to be in control of their learning, rather than any need on their part to have their learning managed by us: we shouldn't do for children what they need to learn for themselves. As parents, we may already have an agenda for them, wanting them to be a certain way or to fulfil our expectations of 'success'. It is much more difficult but so important to respect the child as he is, trusting that, given opportunities to learn, he will take them as he needs to. And through their play – often called the child's 'work' – we have opportunities to enter the child's imaginative world. Lying down together for a midday rest can become a game where we make ourselves comfortable and tell each other stories.

The Great Education Debate

Education has long been polarized into a battle between the 'traditionalists', where the emphasis is on teaching and what is taught, and the 'progressives', who focus on the learner and the learning that can take place when education is 'child-centred' – although, in practice, all shades of the two extremes are to be found. Alexander was very interested in this problem and he saw the answer lying in some kind of middle way:

> Give a child conscious control and you give him poise, the essential starting point for education . . . you fit him for any and every mode of life . . . Without that poise, which is a result aimed at by neither the old nor the

Fig. 151

Fig. 152

Fig. 153

The child moving freely about.

new methods of education, he will presently be cramped and distorted by his environment.[9]

Children's education has undoubtedly suffered in many countries as a result of sea changes in education policy in recent times that deny the stable conditions necessary for thoughtful and patient reform. Many of the changes, which were hurriedly implemented, had little evidence to support their widespread adoption.

The biggest shake-up has been in primary school education, where so much more now has to be taught; many things are thus covered only superficially. So what are the implications for those of us who have a vision of a more holistic education that might be underpinned by an understanding of the Alexander Technique? And how might the Technique have an effect on the content and – more importantly – the approach to subjects such as English (in the learning of basic skills like handwriting, reading and speaking/listening), science (how we work), physical education and music? And what can parents, teachers and children do about it?

Early Childhood

The five-year-old is potentially more poised than the pre-school child. He is just as active, but his movements are more controlled and economical and he is able to maintain a position for longer. However, keeping relatively still may have been achieved by many hours of watching TV, often with the same collapsed posture well-established in older members of the family. Some parents are tempted to nag their children to 'sit up straight'. However well-meaning, if this instruction is responded to (and it may not be except with an annoyed shrug of the shoulders!), it is bound to produce tension and then further slumping as fatigue overcomes the child. In one small study in an American school, it was found that most six- and seven-year-olds could not sit cross-legged without pulling down badly; muscles had already tightened and shortened and 'ageing' was well under way.[10]

A recent study on back pain found that most primary school pupils are sitting at furniture that is the wrong height for them.[11] Chairs, often chosen for ease of stacking purposes, slope backwards and are too low, and tables are too high, but the main problem is that schools do not provide a wide enough range of furniture. Also, the usual classroom design – children working in small groups around the same-sized, level table, needing to twist round when the teacher wants their attention – further works against their maintaining poise and good use. We are creating multitudes of back-sufferers in our living rooms and classrooms. None of this seems to be regarded as a priority. Perhaps this is an issue you would want to raise with your school?

Handwriting

In the teaching of handwriting the focus of attention is usually on the marks on the piece of paper before the child – the *end* – not at all on *how* the child is acquiring the skills of handwriting.

The question why most of us slant the paper on which we are writing has implications for the development of a fluent writing style. This is of fundamental importance both in school and in daily life, and in making writing a source of pleasure and pride. If you look closely at how most people write, you can observe all kinds of muscular tensions out of all proportion to what should, in the end, be the relatively small task of moving a small object – the pen – through small distances. Why, for instance, is the tongue often restless or the jaw clenched? Notice, too, how the right-hander will invariably slant the paper to the left; the head follows to orientate the eyes to the line of writing, and the head and neck are usually poked forward, especially if the writing surface is too low and not slanted up. This produces excessive work in muscles on the right side of the neck and at the nape; the right shoulder hunches more than the left, and tension spreads down the writing arm.

Writing 'grip'   There are all manner of tension-creating grips. The most common is the one usually advocated: that of holding the pen between the pads of the thumb and forefinger, and against the side of the second finger. In informal surveys we have carried out at workshops, it appears that about a third of adults have, or have had, calluses on the second finger of their writing hand: our conclusion is that the recommended grip must be seriously wrong. Using this grip, the hand retracts on the tightening wrist, the fingers and knuckles are white with pressure and the elbow tends to pull in to the side, jamming the upper arm into the shoulder. The movement of the pen is controlled by an unduly flexed thumb, locking the wrist and forcing the pen against the side of the second finger, the first finger being hyperextended.

The craft of handwriting – with a relaxed arm – is one of the basic skills that should and must be taught properly *at the outset*. There is good evidence (in pictures and early handwriting manuals) that this used to be common practice.[12] It is not easy to alter a poor writing grip once established. Infant school teachers and parents, therefore, have an important duty to discharge in this respect, but their first responsibility is to re-examine how they themselves write, if the children in their care are going to have any chance of acquiring good habits. You will discover that if you place the paper level, without slanting it, a little to the right, it is easier on your neck and writing arm. And if you are prepared to experiment with your writing grip, you will discover that, in order to maintain a relatively free writing arm, it is necessary to employ *the pads of the first three fingers*. This needs to take place, of course, in the context of good overall body use facilitated by the proper arrangement of chair and writing surface. (As for writing implements, our opinion is that nothing substitutes satisfactorily for a soft pencil or fibre-tip – but they thicken quickly – or fountain pen: no other instrument can glide so smoothly over the page. Ball-point pens tend to skid and are therefore 'gripped' to prevent untoward movement; and even the new roller-balls tend to scratch.)

To overthrow habits of many years is no easy matter, but if you apply Alexander principles patiently, real progress can be made. You will then find that your elbow leads the hand across the page; the wrist will be more relaxed and gentle movements of all three fingers holding the pen – and the hand – will form your writing. And so the attitude of the forearm will be quite different – at 45 degrees to the paper, making it possible to position the paper straight in front of you, without cramping the arm, and without any need to tilt your head to one side; you are therefore in a virtuous cycle where all parts of the body are doing their share of the work in writing – and no more.

Left-handers have special problems with an alphabet and writing designed for a right-handed world. They frequently try to write with a hooked hand and wrist, which as well as being very tense can lead to smudging. The remedy usually suggested is to slant the paper to the right, but this, of course, leads to the head being held at an awkward angle. Another possibility, which a number of left-handers have fluently demonstrated to us at workshops, is to turn the paper on its side so that predominantly pulling movements of the pen are made vertically down the paper. This may sound very strange, because they have to learn to read down, rather than across, the page, but it appears to be a very successful solution and worth further investigation.

Science

Simple anatomical concepts can be made very relevant and practical. We have previously mentioned two common errors in 'body mapping' in adults: the confusion about the location of hip *joints* compared with hip *bones;* and the tendency to move the shoulder unnecessarily as though it is part of the arm. There are others, and distinctions can be clearly demonstrated to the child, using his own experience and examining a skeleton or looking at an anatomy book. Perhaps the most important misconception is that the joint where the head balances on the neck is perceived to be lower than it actually is: this leads to gross and tense movements of the neck with the head, when, for example, the child is looking down at his work. Being more aware of all these concepts gives the child some choice in the way he uses himself and is empowering knowledge, rather than the memorization of facts for the sake of passing a test. Alexander noted:

> . . . to find out 'how it works' is the natural desire of every healthy child . . . in schools where experiments have been made in re-education on a general basis . . . *they are not slow to recognize that they are the most interesting machines.*[13]

Music

Most music instructors are unaware of the problems inherent in practising an instrument or singing and how children can prepare for and perform music more effectively and enjoyably. Many adults gave up on music because they were 'made' to practise at a young age. If playing music does not give us pleasure, perhaps it's better not to have anything to do with it. Some children would really like to play better, but they improve more slowly than they should: bad habits of practising acquired early on are difficult to change. In particular, 'rushing' at an unfamiliar piece of music – stumbling through it without having created a clear idea of it in your mind, before going near the instrument – is likely to lead to more faltering progress and discouragement in mastering technically demanding pieces.

Some instruments – the violin, viola, saxophone and flute – are especially awkward to play and it would be prudent to give your child some sensitive exposure to the Alexander Technique early in their acquisition of technique: instrumental teachers often do not address the *mechanical* problems sufficiently. For instance, it should be possible to hold the violin gently but firmly in place between the chin and shoulder. It is not necessary to clamp down on the instrument, fixing the head to one side and twisting and compressing the spine. This is partly a matter of habit. 'Willowy' children, however, will need special help with the provision of larger shoulder (or ideally, chin) rests.

Physical Education

The message generally conveyed to children throughout their schooling, from age five to sixteen, is that exercise (particularly aerobic exercise) is good for you. Little mention is made of the *risks* of exercising; or how to judge, in an individual case, whether a certain form of exercising might produce damage which would outweigh any possible benefits.

This, unfortunately, is not common knowledge among teachers of physical education and coaches; here are some recent observations – made by a student teacher who has had Alexander lessons – during her teaching practise:

> A gym lesson for 10-year-olds began with cold children (who had been kept waiting in a corridor) having to do vigorous and fast sit-ups with their feet hooked under the wall-bars! This was their 'warm-up activity' before the lesson proper.[14]

Someone using these methods might well claim that the children don't report injury. A theme of our book, however, is the need to take thoughtful action to *prevent* ills that might otherwise be caused. Just because children don't say they are in pain doesn't mean that: (a) they are not; and (b) damage is not being caused by the cumulative strain – unrecognized in its early stages – that will become evident in adolescence or adult life.

So, what kinds of activity might be encouraged? Ones that children choose themselves, not ones they are coerced into. In general, free movement, folk dancing, walking and swimming should come before more specialized sporting activities. An important aim should be to maintain or recover the manner of bending that the pre-school child naturally and easily employs. The capacity to squat comfortably was a necessary step in the evolution of the poised, erect posture. It might be added that to maintain an erect posture when sitting or standing is greatly aided by the ability to squat easily (quite apart from the implications for child-bearing women). One small survey found that only half of the children in an American elementary school *could* still squat with their heels down, comfortably; one-quarter hunched to prevent falling backwards, heels off the floor.[15] We recently observed a large number of primary school children taking the opportunity to do some ice-skating on a dry rink that had been laid down during half-term in the school hall. Nearly all of them tried to skate in a top-heavy fashion with their leg joints tensely held. By adolescence, harmful habits of bending have become entrenched, although muscles have not yet become irrevocably shortened. *The child who bends well now looks 'abnormal"!*

Adolescence

The growth of bones is rapid in early and middle puberty; muscles have to lengthen accordingly. Interestingly, this stage of development is the opposite of the earlier stage: growth now starts from the most peripheral parts of the body, towards the centre. The fact that the limbs develop in advance of the torso, and hands and feet before upper arms and thighs, accounts for the 'gangliness' of adolescence – quite apart from any malcoordination that will almost certainly be present. So-called 'growing pains', the exact cause of which is apparently not known, can produce disturbing cramp-like pains in the body of muscle, away from joints. At this stage, joints are particularly sensitive and easily inflamed by overuse or repetitive exercise.

Work positions
Schoolchildren are now over 4 in. (10 cm) taller than at the beginning of the twentieth century.[16] Much more time at school is spent seated, reading and writing. Has school furniture for ever-taller youngsters kept pace? Not only have the ergonomic insights of the last century been ignored, but conditions have actually worsened: desks which used to slope are now level; seats which used to be level, sometimes with a passable back support, now slope backwards with a completely inadequate back support. Most chairs in schools are less than the standard height for dining chairs, which at 46 cm (18 in.) will fit someone of only 5 ft (152 cm) but most youngsters – even by eleven or twelve years old – are well above this height.

What a responsibility we have to create conditions which will allow proper growth and development! Anything that produces a cramped

Fig. 154   A slightly forward-tilted, high enough chair and a raised, slanted writing surface can help support a more expanded posture while studying.

posture should be avoided. Furniture should be correctly chosen and arranged. The starting point should be to get the chair right and then to adjust the rest of the 'work-station' accordingly. As a rough guide, chair-seat height (measured from the child's sitting bones on a slightly forward-tilted chair – about 4 degrees) should be one-third the child's height so that the hips will be significantly higher than the knees to help prevent the pelvis tilting back and collapse of the lower spine. Desk height should be about one-half the child's height (measured from the writing surface, sloped at abut 15 degrees) to help avoid the head and neck poking forward and putting pressure on the upper spine (Fig. 154). To make a simple writing slope (angle 15 degrees plus, or an adjustable slope, 15–30 degrees) would be a very valuable project for every child to take on in technology.[17]

When sitting at a computer, the same considerations about a working chair apply; this time, though, the operator will tend to sit more vertically, instead of leaning forwards from the hips to write. The keyboard should be at such a height that the child's forearm is almost parallel to the floor, his elbow very slightly higher than his forearm so that his wrist is in its most neutral position (to help prevent repetitive strain injuries). The top of the screen should be approximately at eye level, so that with his head releasing forward and up off the top of his neck, his eyes will angle a little downwards to read the characters at the centre of the screen, slightly tilted upwards so that his line of vision is perpendicular to the screen (to help prevent neck and shoulder problems and eyestrain).

The school that has its computer room set up to accommodate different sizes of youngsters is very much the exception. Nor are students encouraged to learn keyboarding skills to avoid the tension-creating, jerky movements of the head and eyes between keyboard and screen. To prevent craning the head to the side to see any text to be keyed in, they should be advised to use document holders.

Physical education

It is questionable whether youngsters should be forced to take part in vigorous exercise they do not wish to undertake; this is not a recipe for continuing exercise into adult life.

Is there good evidence for the need to exercise vigorously to protect against heart disease? It is often suggested, for instance, that to exert a training effect on the cardio-vascular system while walking, you should swing small weights at the same time, in order to raise your pulse rate and increase the amount of energy being expended. But the fact is that most of us already make too much effort while walking, with tense legs and excessive pressure on the lower back. Surely a more intelligent approach would be to encourage youngsters to pace themselves better, not to expend energy wastefully? A further consideration is that there is a lot more to preventing heart disease than mindless physical slog: namely, finding an occupation that brings contentment and sustaining heartening personal relations.

Certain physical activities should, in our view, definitely be avoided. These include: weight-lifting and aerobics (the current trend is 'step' classes), often carried out to music that imposes its own pace on the movements, so that the student has little opportunity to register his body's responses; gymnastic exercises that require interference with the primary control; dance that involves repetitive angular movements; and sports that require marked bending and twisting movements of the spine which put harmful stresses on the discs, for example, hockey and squash (youngsters with no family history of back problems, who are of stocky build, may be able to get away with these). The few with special talents may want to exploit them, but the risks of disability – even by early adult life – should be spelled out.

The main problem is that mind and body are treated as though they are separate: physical education is seen, wrongly, as a remedy for the slumped habits of school work. On the one hand, youngsters are not shown how to apply themselves intelligently to their 'physical' activities; and on the other hand, the primary 'instrument' – the body – is given little attention when they concentrate on their 'mental' work.

Alexander's Insights into Education and What it could Be

Alexander started a primary school for children in 1924 in England which continued into the early Second World War years (finally being evacuated to the United States from London). The children who attended usually had learning difficulties of one sort or another. They had private lessons in the Technique (as did their parents) and although the curriculum was of the usual kind for those days, the teaching was carried out by Alexander's assistants. Unfortunately, there is no detailed appraisal of his educational experiment in the available literature, but its longevity without state support perhaps implies that it was reasonably successful. Before we give you a flavour of what is known of the 'little school', we shall outline Alexander's aim in setting it up and consider some of his ideas on the *process* of education.

Alexander noted how children who came for lessons and were then thrust back into the normal school environment (quite repressive by modern standards) were not getting a fair chance of carrying through into their daily activities the changes made in their use during lessons. The pivotal insight he had into the failure of most educational enterprise is highlighted in his statement of intent regarding the 'little school' he had set up:

> ... the end for which [the children in class] are working is of minor importance as compared with the way they direct the use of themselves for the gaining of that end.[18] [our italics]

End-gaining or means-whereby?
Alexander noted how, when an imperfectly coordinated child is asked to do something new (for example in handwriting), he will invariably show signs of strain in his attempts to be 'right': tense posture, held breath, fixed expression, impaired concentration – and he will tire quickly. Furthermore, 'every unsuccessful "try" not only reinforces the pupil's old wrong psychophysical habits associated with his conception of a particular act, but involves at the same time new emotional experiences of discouragement, worry, fear, and anxiety.'[19] If, instead, Alexander argued, attention is given to *how* the child is to aquire a certain skill, he will not be asked to do something until there is a fair chance of success; then, any failure will be taken in his stride as a valuable learning experience. It might be added that, if the child were to be more in charge of his own learning, he would be less inclined to make unreasonable demands on himself; the task, then, of the teacher is to be alert to the signs of misuse, and to give help and guidance when the child's efforts to achieve his ends are becoming excessive.

Inhibition and non-doing

This is the ability, as you will recall, of refusing to be immediately impelled into action, so that there is the opportunity for calm reflection on what is to be attempted and how best to achieve it. Alexander observed that children start school 'with poor equipment on the inhibitory side'; and that, during their schooling, the balance between volition and inhibition is tipped even further in favour of volition. Perhaps this is even more the case nowadays, with the pressures of information overload as well as anxieties about finding a place in a profoundly disturbing and fast-moving world. Inhibition – 'the will not to do' – must come prior to action, 'the will-to-do', otherwise there is nothing to maintain integrity and prevent the dissipation of the child's energies in too many and, perhaps, inappropriate directions. This presupposes some development of self-awareness on the part of the child: Margaret Donaldson, in her classic study of the development of children's minds, says, 'If a child is going to control and direct his own thinking . . . he must become conscious of it.'[20]

Sensory appreciation

We rely on our kinaesthetic sense to guide us in all our activities. If this sense is not registering accurately, then it 'interferes with the child's natural coordination in skill-learning of all kinds, in much the same way that impairment of other senses, such as sight and hearing, can create learning problems'.[21] This fundamental insight is barely addressed by mainstream educators and yet its neglect has so many ramifications for all aspects of child development and functioning.

The 'Little School'

Irene Tasker, Montessori and Alexander-trained, said that of all the work she did with the children at the 'little school', the application of the Alexander Technique to speaking contributed more than anything to their improvement as a whole. Here is part of an account of her work, as it was carried out in the 1920s:

> . . . inhibition and the orders [directions] given to prevent wrong use were taught, discussed and practised during the pupils' rest periods; and, later, applied to all their work and games. For instance, an end-of-term play would be prepared by these methods. Dramatic situations, and difficulties such as problems of presentation, words and their meaning, were all thoroughly considered. Each child learnt the whole play as he rested on his back and kept the orders going, so that his use for memory, and any emotion suggested by the play, was being gradually built into a total pattern of activity. He learnt to inhibit the immediate reaction to noise or interruption.
>
> This work would go on for most of the term and only a fortnight or so before the production date would the children, quite spontaneously, go into action. By that time there was very little for the producer to do, for character and situation were so thoroughly integrated. Miss Tasker told of

a delightful incident in an outdoor performance of *A Midsummer Night's Dream*, when a noisy plane circled low over the garden, completely drowning the actors' voices. The small Titania was quite unperturbed and, with her finger to her lips, held the situation for three solid minutes till the intruder had flown off. Then the children resumed the play quite calmly as if nothing had happened.[22]

Although Alexander intended to re-open his school after the Second World War, the experiment came to a close. There were practical reasons: the site had been bomb-damaged but perhaps the main reason was that Alexander, now in his 70s, was caught up in a libel action he had brought; although he was successful, the action dragged on for nearly four years.

Other projects

Various attempts have been made since the 'little school' to apply aspects of Alexander's ideas to the existing system, with mixed results. It has been said that you cannot *apply* Alexander's key ideas – they have to be *lived*. But a number of attempts have been made, in England, South Africa and the United States, which furnish insights for parents and teachers into the potential of the Alexander Technique to aid children's learning.

Jack Fenton, retired headmaster and lecturer in physical and health education, set up a number of projects over twenty years ago that ran for some months in primary and secondary schools in England. He found the children receptive to ideas about body use and its effects, the teachers less so. His book, *Choice of Habit*,[23] has lots of useful suggestions for teachers – particularly physical education teachers – on the practical importance of a vision of poised and free movement as a basis for *all* a school child's activities.

Another experiment showed striking benefits of the value of the Technique, applied in an intensive way, with a group of children who were having reading difficulties. During their summer holidays they chose to participate in a special three-week programme at their school. Jean Shepherd, the Alexander teacher involved, provided reading-rests to hold their books and gave each child help in finding a more poised sitting position. The children were asked to be aware of the information coming to them from their senses and, when they were really *present*, to start focusing on their reading books. Jean describes what happened next:

> From then on, it was simple Alexander principle: *stop, think and act*. I gave them lots of time; reading a phrase for them – they following it, reading it for themselves and, later on, one by one, 'Could you read that back? No – well, it doesn't matter. Read it again . . . Could you *now*? Not sure? When you know you're sure, when you know you can give it back to me, then you give it back to me . . . Are you sure?' 'Yes'. Out it came, confidently, no stumbling. We went round the class like this – stop, think and act – plenty of time – it doesn't matter, nothing matters – but don't speak until you feel confident enough to, and it doesn't matter then if you make a mistake. We'll succeed *in the end* – they were so pleased to be able to do it.

> I used to give the children the example of a cat. Watch a cat as it sits waiting to jump onto a post. It really knows where it is, where it's going and then moves. It doesn't flap about in mid-air. It just gets on with it.[24]

At the end of the three weeks, the children, previously defiant and restless, were calm and contented, all having achieved significant improvement in their reading ability; some of the children had attained the average reading competence for their age group.

Fenton encouraged the start-up of another project which was funded by the Back Pain Association in 1982, the aim being to provide education for primary school children in order to protect them against back pain in later years. The project was fraught with difficulties from the start, not least of which were poorly designed chairs and tables which militated against maintaining good use while the children were reading and writing; and the fact that some of the teachers involved expected instant results – immediate application in the classroom, without any commitment on their part. Sue Thame, who ran the project, was pessimistic in her summing up about any chance of large-scale change in the state system: the only hope, in her view, lay with individual teachers working with their own classes of children, preferably in independently funded schools where the Alexander Technique could be part of a commitment to a more holistic kind of education.[25]

Ann Mathews, a school-teacher who subsequently trained in the Alexander Technique, documented a wealth of observations and insights on the benefits of bringing a profound 'Alexander awareness' to the classroom in the American school system in the early 1980s, with benefits for teachers, children and even the children's families. Her basic proposition was that

> *children would be more aware, more integrated, and incidentally learn better, if in the process they do not lose that delicate awareness of balance and efficient Use of the whole organism that they have achieved unaided in gaining the upright human stature.* [26][our italics]

She had begun having Alexander lessons to cope with the 'numbing fatigue' of her first year of teaching; stress-related symptoms had been attributed to external factors such as difficult children, new job, commuting and so, but it hadn't occurred to her that there was anything wrong with her posture or coordination. As her own use gradually improved, she began to see the children quite differently. One of the first stories she recounts is of a colleague:

> A teacher calls her six- and seven-year-olds to gather round her on the floor and listen to a story. Most sit cross-legged with their spines collapsed and their heads pulled back onto their necks as they look up at the teacher. One boy is kneeling close to the teacher, back beautifully aligned, head balancing on the top. 'You are blocking the people behind you', says the teacher, in a reproachful tone. 'Sit down so that they can see the picture.' The child sits down obediently and collapses like the others around him.

The teacher does not see what has happened, does not see that she has required the child to go from a poised, balanced, alert position, to one that is cramped and distorted. Knowing better than to protest, the child looks resigned.[27]

Later on, she began observing things about the children she was teaching:

I began noticing how frequently the children adopted tense postures when asking permission to do things, even when the clear expectation was that the answer from me would be Yes. They would look up at me and hunch their shoulders up towards their ears . . . The more I became aware of their behaviour the more fully I sensed how tense and anxious a position it was, and the more I realized that they were quite oblivious of what they were doing to themselves. I would frequently go down to their level, sitting or kneeling, and put my two hands on their shoulders. The shoulders would drop, their faces would relax, and their voices would soften. They appeared to welcome this unspoken help in releasing the unnecessary tension. *I began to wonder what it might be like to have a classroom in which tense awkward mannerisms were at a minimum rather than a chronic presence.*[28] [our italics]

Ann Mathews describes one project where she began by giving individual work on a weekly basis to the teachers and to any of the primary-school-age youngsters who signed up for it:

One day Joyce [one of the teachers] told me she had been noticing the younger children to whom she was teaching cursive writing. 'Whenever they are trying hard,' she said, 'they start to pull down and hunch over. I reminded them of what you would say and some of them changed at the thought, but I decided to go round and try to give them the same sort of guidance you do. It was a funny thing. The ones who work with you regularly just floated up at the lightest touch, but the others fell into two categories: either they were as heavy as stone and I had no idea what you would do when confronted with this, or they jerked up suddenly and sat there looking all braced and military, which I was sure were not what you get either in them or in me.'[29]

Ann reflects on her difficulties in becoming more aware of her own use, but describes a turning point when she was attempting to give special help to Michael, a child with a reading problem:

I was cheering him on with words of encouragement. Gradually I became aware of my own use: shoulders contracted, ribs still, face muscles overworking to show enthusiasm and support – it felt terrible. I tried to inhibit the contraction, I gave the orders to release, lengthen and widen and serenity was restored. But I kept feeling the impulse to tighten again and again as if *this was teaching* – exhausting myself to give to another.

   . . . the significance of the hour with Michael dawned on me. This is what I used to do in the classroom all the time, and never was aware of it. When I was expressing encouragement, interest, excitement, affection – in other words all the things I thought were part and parcel of my creativity as a teacher – I was also conveying unbelievable amounts of tension. No wonder I had been so exhausted all the time.[30]

Shortly after this Ann started full-time training to be a teacher of the Alexander Technique and, a year later, went back to class teaching for a term, on this occasion with nine-year-olds who were notoriously resourceful in testing new teachers. She was uncertain how to begin, but then decided to start experimenting with 'likely' subjects:

> I approached a pair of very docile little girls who always hovered around teacher, eager for interaction, during an indoor recess. I said 'Would you like me to see whether your heads can balance freely on the end of your spines?' They would indeed . . . After balancing their heads, I had them both lie on their backs on the floor with their knees up, and took their heads in my hands to give them a sense of the lengthening spine.
>
> Watching these proceedings, which the girls evidently enjoyed, two other girls asked for a turn, and then a very timid little boy. The next time we did this, there was a request for a turn from some more independent girls and some more of the boys. At this point I had a stroke of luck. The acknowledged leader of the class, an intelligent boy who was comfortable with himself and friendly to others, and incidentally beautifully coordinated and good at sports, asked what I had been doing with the other children. I explained that most people fall into habits of doing simple everyday things in a tense, inefficient way, and then when we want to learn a special skill such as playing a musical instrument, these habits get in our way . . . And if, on the other hand, we already have the ease and control, but have never thought about it because we could always count on this being so, it can be interesting to understand why our coordination is so good and reliable. The boy was immediately interested and asked for a turn. The usually diffident, if not hostile, group of school-haters were watching this scene with undisguised interest and immediately complained that they had not been given a turn. I obliged, and from then on, whenever we had free time in the room the whole lot would get down on the floor and allow me to work with them.[31]

Ann was amazed to discover how readily – on so many levels – the children responded to Alexander work (even with someone who was only a third of the way through her training course):

> I had worked for a few minutes on the floor with a boy who was constantly victimized by the tougher boys in the class and scorned by the girls. His stooped posture, caved-in chest and cringing attitude reflected his experience in the class and doubtless at home as well.
>
> Lying down [in semi-supine] . . . had straightened his habitually stooped spine and widened his shoulders. Several of the usually scornful girls, waiting for their turns, looked down at him. Instead of mocking as they might have done, one said, in a tone of surprise, 'Dylan looks handsome.' Her companions agreed. I pointed out that, when they lie in this position, they are doing nothing at all, *they are simply allowing themselves to be*, as Dylan was, at the moment, simply being. I reminded him that we all have little tightening habits, most of which we are unaware of, and that

his habit, like many other people's, was to sit hunched over. People come to think of him as being that shape, but it is not true . . . he can choose not to do it. Here we see how he really is.

The relaxed child did indeed look beautiful. The girls were, for once, without words, and the boy was listening.[32]

One example of this natural perceptiveness of children was shown one day while Ann was working with an eight-year-old child in the 'semi-supine' position:

With a number of six- to nine-year-olds watching, I gently moved the child's knee from side to side with my fingertips over an arc of about three or four inches. The child was relaxed, letting her leg be moved and neither helping nor hindering, clearly absorbed in sensing the leg going in and out of balance.

On impulse, I looked up at the onlookers. 'Is she moving her leg or am I?' I asked. 'You are,' answered a seven-year-old. 'How do you know?' 'Because it looks different when she does it.'

George Bernard Shaw wrote humorously, 'Mr Alexander calls upon the world to witness a change so small that only he can see it.' But these changes are readily discernible by any Alexander teacher and any student of the Technique who has had sufficient re-education. The seven-year-old 'knew' all about it from her own experience, and could empathize with what her friend was experiencing. She was aware of a fundamental difference in the two kinds of happening, Allowing and Doing. I was impressed. I had not told them to try and tell the difference. My question had been completely spontaneous and had taken them by surprise. The reason I asked it was that I had a sudden hunch that, *although a malcoordinated adult would be unlikely to catch the difference, a child might simply see it, and she had.*[33] [our italics]

Another story is of nine-year-old Thomas, who had been put back a year because of reading difficulties; a tall child, he sagged most of the time and his back was very curved. He seemed fascinated by the Alexander Technique:

One day we were discussing the kinds of feelings that might pull us down . . . In this class I deliberately thought of something that was sad to me, and felt how that might have pulled me down physically, and gave in to it. I asked the children what they saw and was told, 'you got littler', 'your spine curved', 'your head dropped', and so forth. One child said, hesitantly, 'You looked a little sad . . . ' after which there was a torrent of discussion about the kinds of things that had made the children sad in one way or another.

At the end, Thomas said, looking puzzled, 'But Mrs Mathews, when you showed us feeling sad and going down, I felt my spine pulled down.' That took me utterly by surprise. Several hands went up. It is something to think about.[34]

Perhaps a real test of introducing new ideas into the classroom is to see whether the children realize their relevance for themselves. Although she had not suggested or even hinted that their growing awareness of use should be applied outside the classroom, Ann noted that children frequently reported having 'Alexandered' members of their families:

> they tell of listening to a parent complaining of an aching back and saying, 'Daddy, what do you expect? You're sitting all hunched over. Do you want me to lengthen you up?[35]

What You Can Do

(a) The first thing to consider is taking lessons in the Alexander Technique so that you can understand more about your own use and misuse, quite apart from any benefits for the children in your care, whether you are a parent or a teacher. Many teachers are parents too, and the Technique can help you cope better with the stresses of both jobs, as well as maintaining your health and well-being.

(b) Your growing awareness and sensitivity to other people's patterns of misuse (a straight back may have been judged a good thing, whereas now it may be seen to be stiff and rigid) will give you more insight into why youngsters are not functioning well or even failing.

(c) However modest your attempts to share what you know about the Alexander Technique – assuming you do not try to *impose* your enthusiasms! – they are generally welcomed and appreciated by children. Two practical measures can be of benefit: first, encourage your youngster to have a short rest in the semi-supine position before undertaking homework; and second, with their active cooperation and help, get their chair and desk set up as well as possible so that they have less reason to slump after a tiring day at school.

Some of the children in Ann Mathews' study mentioned their difficulties with change: six-year-olds complained of pain when trying to maintain an improved use of themselves. (With adolescents and adults, 'change pains' – associated with a shift in muscular work through the body – can occur and are a transitory phase of learning the Alexander Technique.) Ann points out the disturbing implications of this phenomenon: that pain, which normally signals something is wrong, can serve to perpetuate misuse.

If you are concerned about your primary school age child, let him share a small part of your lessons, *as he wants to*. Adolescents can benefit greatly from a course of lessons for themselves, especially if problems are arising. Even the experience of a few lessons at this stage, if made enjoyable, can plant a seed which may flourish later and in the meantime can be a valuable resource for mitigating, perhaps even preventing, some of the maladjustments of adolescence.

In 1923, John Dewey wrote about the contrast between our increasing technological sophistication and our lack of understanding of ourselves. At the end of our troubled century, his remarks seem ever more pertinent:

> Through modern science we have mastered to a wonderful extent the use of things as tools for accomplishing results upon and through other things. The result is all but a universal state of confusion, discontent and strife. The one factor which is the primary tool in the use of all these other tools, namely ourselves . . . has not even been studied as the central instrumentality . . .
>
> It is, however, one thing to teach the need of a return to the individual man as the ultimate agency in whatever mankind and society can collectively accomplish . . . It is another thing to discover the concrete procedure by which this greatest of all tasks can be executed. And this indispensable thing is exactly what Mr Alexander has accomplished.[36]

Notes

Chapter 1

1 M Wagner, 'Child health care in the 1990's', *Midwife, Health Visitor & Community Nurse* 1990, *26*, 420–2.
2 JE Goldthwaite et al, *Body Mechanics,* Lippincott, 1932.
3 N Tinbergen, 'Ethology and stress disease (Nobel Prize Oration)', *Science* 1974, *185*, 22–7.

Chapter 2

1 JE Goldthwaite et al, *Body Mechanics*, Lippincott, 1932, p. 113.
2 See, DJP Barker (ed), 'Fetal and infant origins of adult disease.' *British Medical Journal,* 1992.
3 On these aspects see J Raphael-Leff, *Psychological Processes of Childbearing,* Chapman-Hall, 1990.
4 See J Drake, *Body Know-How: A Practical Guide to the Use of the Alexander Technique in Everyday Life,* Thorsons, 1991, p. 133.
5 B Conable, *How to Learn the Alexander Technique,* Andover Road Press, 1990.
6 For further details see D Gorman, The Body Moveable, Vol. 3, 1981, pp. 168–9.
7 A good example is L Nilsson, *A Child is Born,* Rev. edn, Dell, 1986.
8 W Barlow, *The Alexander Principle,* Gollancz, 1990, p. 216.

Chapter 3

1 See G Justus Hofmeyr, 'Breech presentation and abnormal lie in late pregnancy', in M Enkin et al. *Effective Care in Pregnancy and Childbirth,* OUP, 1989, pp. 653–5.
2 For a comprehensive discussion of this topic, see E Noble, *Essential Exercises for the Childbearing Year,* John Murray, 1978.
3 For more details, see S Hoare, 'How to avoid an unnecessary episiotomy', in R Claxton (ed), *Birth Matters,* Unwin, 1986.

Chapter 4

1 *Rupture of the Membranes in Labour: A Survey Conducted by the National*

Childbirth Trust, NCT booklet, 1989.

2   L Fenwick and P Simkin, 'Maternal positioning to prevent or alleviate dystocia in labour', *Clinical Obstetrics and Gynecology*, 1987, 30, 83–9.

3   On the effects of these drugs, see National Childbirth Trust Information Sheets, *Epidural Anaesthesia*, June 1991; *The Use of Pethidine in Labour*, January 1989. These are summaries of results of medical research, with extensive bibliography. See also J Priest, *Drugs in Pregnancy and Childbirth*, Pandora, 1990.

4   LE Mehl, 'Psychophysiological aspects of childbirth', in L Feher, *The Psychology of Birth*, Souvenir Press, London, 1980, pp. 40–1.

5   See M Odent, *Birth Reborn*, Souvenir Press, 1984, pp. 121–2. More recent research has tended to confirm Odent's hypothesis.

6   Odent, *Birth Reborn*.

7   L Fenwick and P Simkin, *'Maternal positioning'*.

8   FM Alexander, *The Use of the Self*, Centerline Press, 1984, p. 113.

9   J Roeber, *Shared Parenthood*, Century, 1987, p. 18.

10   These are summarized in M Odent, *Water and Sexuality*, Arcana, 1990.

11   E Noble, *Childbirth with Insight*, Houghton Mifflin, 1983, pp. 77ff.

12   For a comprehensive discussion of syntometrine, see S Inch, *Birthrights*, Greenprint, 1989. Also Priest, *Drugs in pregnancy and childbirth*.

Chapter 6

1   FM Alexander, *Constructive Conscious Control of the Individual*, Centerline Press, 1986 (reprint of 1923 edn), p. 291

2   W Barlow, *The Alexander Principle*, Arrow, 1975, pp. 152–5.

3   *Physical Education in the National Curriculum*, HMSO, 1992.

4   Schools Health Education Unit at Exeter University,*Young People in 1992: A Survey* reported in the *Sunday Times*, 28 Feb 1993.

5   P Macdonald, *The Alexander Technique: As I See it*, Rahula Books, 1989, p. 11.

6   J. Dewey, foreword to FM Alexander, *The Use of The Self*, Gollancz, 1985.

7   J Holt, *How Children Fail*, Penguin.

8   For much of the developmental information described in this chapter, we have drawn from R Lansdown and M Walker, *Your Child's Development*, Frances Lincoln, 1991.

9   FM Alexander, *Man's Supreme Inheritance*, Centerline Press, pp. 81–2.

10   A Mathews, *Implications for Education in the Work of FM Alexander: An Exploratory Project in a Public School Classroom*, unpublished thesis for MSc in Education, Bank Street College of Education, 1984, p. 38. Ann would be delighted to hear from anyone who has done other work in this area or who is particularly interested. Please write to her at 260 Sickletown Rd, Orangeburgh, NY 10962, USA.

11   *The Times Educational Supplement*, 5 Feb 1993, reported on the National Back Pain Association study due to be published in the journal *Ergonomics*.

12   See, for example, the following paintings: *Kit's Writing Lesson*, by Martineau (1826–69); *Erasmus*, by Metsys and Holbein; drawings in Jarman C, *The Development of Handwriting Skills*, Blackwell, 1979, pp. 100 and 120, and description of writing grip on p. 115.

13   Alexander, *Constructive Conscious Control*, p. 291.

14   L Gillard, personal communication.
15   Mathews, *Implications for Education*, p. 39.
16   Much of the thinking behind 'active sitting' derives from the work of AC Mandal, *The Seated Man*, Dafnia Publications, Denmark, 1985.
17   J Drake, *Body Know-How: A Practical Guide to the Use of the Alexander Technique in Everyday Life*, Thorsons, 1991.
18   Alexander, *The Use of the Self*, Appendix.
19   Alexander, *Constructive Conscious Control*, p. 209.
20   M Donaldson, *Children's Minds*, Fontana, 1978, p. 94.
21   Mathews, *Implications for Education*, p. 5.
22   I Tasker, *Connecting Links*, Sheildrake Press, 1978, p. 22; J Warrack, 'Irene Tasker on Education without End-gaining', *Alexander Journal*, 1968, *6*, 4.
23   J Fenton, *Choice of Habit*, Macdonald and Evans, 1973.
24   J Shepherd, in *Making our Links with Children's Education*, eight talks from the 1988 Alexander World Congress at Brighton.
25   Ibid.
26   Mathews, *Implications for Education*, p. 5.
27   Ibid, p. 12.
28   Ibid, p. 23.
29   Mathews, *Implications for Education*, p. 29.
30   Ibid, p. 25.
31   Ibid, pp. 25–6.
32   Ibid, pp. 26–7.
33   Ibid, pp. 28–9.
34   Ibid, pp. 41–2.
35   Ibid, p. 42.
36   J Dewey, foreword to Alexander, *Constructive Conscious Control*.

Further Reading

On the Alexander Technique

Here is a highly selected list of books on the Alexander Technique. We have tried to include books that make an original contribution or that are authoritative sources of information.

Introductory books
Barlow, W, *The Alexander Principle*, Arrow 1990.
Drake, J, *Thorsons Introductory Guide to the Alexander Technique*. Thorsons, 1993.
Drake, J, *Body Know-How: A Practical Guide to the Use of the Alexander Technique in Everyday Life*, Thorsons, 1991.
Gelb, M, *Body Learning*, Arum Press, 1987.

About Alexander and his work
Jones, FP, *Body Awareness in Action: A Study of the Alexander Technique*, Schocken, 1976.
Westfeldt, L, *F Matthias Alexander: The Man and his Work*, Centerline Press, 1986.

Alexander's writings
Maisel, E, ed, *Alexander Technique – the Essential Writings of Matthias Alexander*, 1989. Contains, amongst other key passages, the first chapter of *The Use of the Self*. 'The Evolution of the Technique' ('The Australian Story').

See also the four books by FM Alexander: *Man's Supreme Inheritance, Constructive Conscious Control of the Individual, The Use of the Self, The Universal Constant in Living*. They go in and out of print; publishers are Gollancz in UK, Centerline Press in USA.

On pregnancy and childbirth

Claxton, R, *Birth Matters*, Unwin, 1986.
Dick-Read, G, *Childbirth without Fear*, 5th edn, Harper & Row, 1985.
Enkin, M and others, eds, *A Guide to Effective Care in Pregnancy and Childbirth*, OUP, 1989.
Flint, C, *Sensitive Midwifery*, Heinemann, 1986.
Gaskin, IM, *Spiritual Midwifery*, The Book Publishing Co., 1978.
Inch, S, *Birthrights*, Green Print, 1989.

Inch, S, *Approaching Birth*, Green Print, 1989.

Kitzinger, S, *The Experience of Childbirth*, 5th edn, Penguin, 1984.

Kitzinger, S, *Giving Birth, How it Really Feels*, Gollancz, 1987.

Kitzinger, S, *Home Birth*, Dorling Kindersley, 1991.

Kitzinger, S, *Pregnancy and Childbirth*, rev. edn, Penguin, 1989; Alfred A. Knopf Inc.

Lewison, H, for the NCT, *Your Choices for Childbirth*, Ebury Press, 1991

Noble, E, *Childbirth with Insight*, Houghton Mifflin, 1983

Odent, M, *Birth Reborn*, Souvenir Press, 1984.

Tew, M, *Safer Childbirth?*, Chapman & Hall, 1990; Singular Publishing Group.

Tucker, G, *The NCT Book of Pregnancy, Birth and Parenthood*, OUP 1992.

On breastfeeding

Kitzinger, S, *Breastfeeding your Baby*, Dorling Kindersley, 1989; Alfred A. Knopf Inc.

Smale, M, *The NCT Book of Breastfeeding*, Vermilion, 1992.

Appendix 1

Labour Reminder: some suggestions

First stage

- Move in a relaxed way. Listen to your body's signals: when you recognize that a contraction is about to begin, meet it with your directions and breathe out.
- Take a bath/shower, visit the loo (bathroom) often. Keep a balance between rest and activity; crawl. Notice the length of contractions and of intervals between them. Build up a mental picture of dilation. Breathe naturally and comfortably. From time to time renew your directions.
- Eat light meals*; drink plenty**. Play music.
- *When contractions get stronger*, change position: knees; all fours; lunge against wall, furniture or with partner. Keep upright. Vary your movements: from standing to kneeling to half squat, to full squat, and back to standing. Rock together in monkey or lunge; crawl.
- Release: neck, forehead; unclench hands and teeth; produce saliva and keep your mouth soft; swallow. Drop shoulders. Ease feet. Talk to baby. Massage: lower back, thighs, tummy with soft fingertips. Cuddle; hold hands; keep eye contact. Renew your directions. Rest on cushion or gymnastic ball.
- When in doubt – blow out. Whisper 'ah'.
- If dizzy, breathe through cupped hands. Suck ice cubes, take small sips of water. Eat if you are hungry.

Transition

- Encouragement: you are nearly there! Distraction techniques if needed, e.g. counting backwards. Change position. Knee-chest position if premature urge to push. Lying on side; squatting; sit on a ball or facing the back of a simple kitchen chair. Massage with ball; massage feet. Try another bath or shower. Renew your directions. Accept changes of mood and intensity of contractions.

*Soup, sandwiches, fruit.
** Tea, herbal tea with honey (good for energy), water.

Second stage

- Try upright positions, supported squat, kneeling. No clenching. Breathe the baby out as you bear down. Don't hesitate to moan and groan if you want to. Pant slowly when head is born. Relax mouth and jaws. Touch baby's head if you like.

Third Stage

- Pick up your baby and hold close to you. For physiological third stage, stay upright. For managed third stage, recline.

Things you may find useful

sponge
ice-pack
water spray
ice-cubes
oil for massage
socks
ball

small cushions
a foam mat
camera
music
food* and drink**
T-shirts for you and partner

Congratulations!

Appendix 2

Useful addresses

Alexander Technique Professional Organizations

The following will provide lists of teachers who have completed the three years of an approved training course (please send a stamped, addressed envelope).

UK
The Society of Teachers of the Alexander Technique (STAT)
20 London House
266 Fulham Road
London SW10 9EL
Tel: (071) 351 0828

Australia
Australian Society of Teachers of the Alexander Technique (AUSTAT)
PO Box 716
Darlinghurst
NSW 2010

Canada
Canadian Society of Teachers of the Alexander Technique (CANSTAT)
Box 502, Station E
Montreal H2T 3A9
Tel: (514) 598 8879

Denmark
Danish Society of Teachers of the Alexander Technique (DFLAT)
c/o Mary McGovern
Sandhojen 18
DK-2720, Vanlose
Tel: (31) 741366

Germany
German Society of Teachers of the Alexander Technique (GLAT)
Postfach 5312
7800 Freiburg
Tel: (0761) 475995

Israel
Israeli Society of Teachers of the Alexander Technique (ISTAT)
c/o Nelken
26 Radak Street
Jerusalem
Tel: (02) 660683

The Netherlands
The Netherlands Society of Teachers of the Alexander Technique
Max Havelaanaan 80
1183 HN Amstelveen
Tel: (020) 439052

South Africa
South African Society of Teachers of the Alexander Technique (SASTAT)
35 Thornhill Rd
Rondebosch 7700
Tel: (021) 686 8454

Switzerland
Swiss Society of Teachers of the Alexander Technique (SVLAT)
Postfach
CH-8032 Zurich

USA
North American Society of Teachers of the Alexander Technique (NASTAT)
Box 3992
Champaign
IL 61826-3992
Tel: (217) 359 3529

There are also qualified teachers in Argentina, Austria, Belgium, Brazil, Colombia, Finland, France, Hong Kong, Iceland, Irish Republic, Italy, Japan, Luxembourg, Mexico, New Zealand, Norway, Pakistan, Poland, Seychelles, Spain and Sweden. Contact STAT (address and phone number above) for further details.

Other useful addresses

National Childbirth Trust (NCT)
Alexandra House
Oldham Terrace
London W3 6NH
Tel: (081) 992 8637

NCT Maternity Sales
Burnfield Avenue
Glasgow
G46 7TL
Tel: (041) 633 5552

Association for Improvements in the Maternity Services (AIMS)
Sandar Warshal
40 Kingswood Avenue
London NW6 6LS
Tel: (081) 960 5585

Association of Radical Midwives (ARM)
62 Greetby Hill
Ormskirk
Lancs
L32 2DT
Tel: (0695) 721777

Eutokia Alexander classes for pregnant women
5 Milman Road
London NW6 6EN
Tel: (081) 969 5356

Homebirth Movement
22 Anson Road
London N7 0RD

Independent Midwives Association
Nightingale Cottage
Shamblehurst Lane
Botley, Hants. SO3 2BY

Maternity Alliance
15 Britannia St
London WC1X 9JP
Tel: (071) 837 1265

Society to Support Home Confinement
Lydgate, Lydgate Lane
Wolsingham
Bishop Aukland
Co. Durham DL13 3HA
Tel: (09565) 528044

Glossary

Active birth   An approach to childbirth in which the woman keeps upright, uses yoga-based positions and is encouraged to move freely during labour.

Active management of labour   Constant technological monitoring and medical intervention during labour.

Adrenalin   A hormone that causes constriction of the arteries, raised blood pressure and quickening of the pulse.

Amniotic fluid (waters)   The colourless fluid surrounding the baby within the membrane in the uterus.

Anterior lip   A fold of skin that sometimes remains in the rim of the cervix in front of the baby's head as a result of uneven dilation of the cervix during the first stage of labour. Eventually the cervix dilates fully and the lip disappears.

Anterior presentation   The preferred position of the baby during birth: the back of its head faces the mother's front.

ARM   Artificial rupture of the membrane surrounding the baby in the uterus.

Body sense   See *Kinaesthetic sense*

Breech presentation   Head-up position of the baby before birth.

Caesarean section   Delivery of the baby through a surgical cut in the mother's abdomen and uterus.

Catecholamines   A group of chemicals secreted by the body, together with adrenalin, in times of fear and stress. They work against oxytocin and may depress uterine activity.

Cervix   The neck of the uterus.

Conscious control   The constructive self-guidance of the person in all her activities, using herself well as a whole in whatever she does, through having a clear idea of the movement required and employing inhibition and direction-giving/sending.

Direction-giving/sending   The process of projecting messages from the brain to the primary control ('let the neck be free, to let the head go forward

175

and up, to let the back lengthen and widen') and secondary directions to the limbs, to facilitate improved coordination.

Dynamic   The term applied to position, relaxation and movement to imply an active release of undue tension, creating a more expanded posture.

End-gaining versus means-whereby   The compulsion to strive for our ends – never mind the costs in failure, strain and fatigue – as opposed to the intelligent application of our minds to find more efficient and effective ways of achieving our goals.

Endorphins   The body's natural painkilling hormones whose chemical structure resembles that of morphine.

Epidural anaesthetic   Anaesthetic injected into the lower part of the spine. If administered well it eliminates the pain of contractions. The woman has to stay in bed.

Episiotomy   Cut made in the perineum to enlarge the passageway for the baby.

Foetal heart monitor   A machine that registers the baby's heartbeat using a belt fastened to the mother's abdomen, or an electrode inserted through the vagina and clipped to the baby's head. The latter can only be done after the membranes have ruptured.

Induction   Causing labour to start artificially.

Inhibition and non-doing   Attending to the 'means whereby': the temporary refusal to react automatically to a stimulus so that we do not 'get set' for an activity in a harmful way, allowing the opportunity for a new, reasoned and creative response, prior to and accompanied by direction giving.

Kinaesthetic sense   (*kinesis* = movement, *aesthesis* = sensation) Body sense, the 'lost' sixth sense. Alexander drew our attention to the serious impairment of our 'sensory appreciation' – faulty patterns of use come to feel right and we are often quite unable to distinguish between appropriate muscle tone and extensive tension in our activities.

Lunge   One of Alexander's 'positions of mechanical advantage', involving a powerful weight transfer forwards or backwards, facilitated by a coordinated leg thrust. Combined with monkey it creates a flexible base for lifting movements.

Means-whereby   See *End-gaining versus means-whereby.*

Medau Rhythmic Movement   A method of rhythmic movement accompanied by music, developed by Hinrich Medau (1890-1974). It seeks to promote creative artistic powers. The emphasis is on movement of the whole body in a continuous flow, using hand-held apparatus such as balls, clubs and hoops.

Monkey   One of Alexander's 'positions of mechanical advantage'; a way of bending with a variable degree of forward tilt around the hip joints, while maintaining the neck-head-back relationship and free use of the arms.

Muscle tone   The amount of mechanical tension in muscles: the Alexander Technique helps us find a better balance between too much and too little muscular work, as well as allowing a proper distribution of tone in different parts of the body, necessary for carrying out a given activity in an economical way.

Neck-head-back relationship   See *Primary Control.*

Occiput   The back of the skull

Oedema   Accumulation of fluid in body tissue; for example, in the feet, ankles or hands.

OP   See *Posterior presentation.*

Oxytocin   A hormone that stimulates uterine contractions and the production of milk.

Pethidine   A synthetic narcotic analgesic usually given as intramuscular injection. The drug changes the perception of pain rather than eliminating it altogether. The woman will be advised to stay in bed.

Placenta   A sponge-like organ attached to the wall of the uterus, through which the baby is connected to its mother's bloodstream.

Posterior presentation (OP)   Position of the baby during birth, in which the back of its head faces the mother's back.

Primary control   Alexander's (re)discovery that a certain dynamic relationship between neck, head and back helps overall coordination: the head balances delicately on top of a relatively free neck, allowing the spine to lengthen and the torso to widen, improving body mechanics as a whole.

Progesterone   A female sex hormone that prepares the uterus for the fertilized egg and maintains pregnancy.

Prostaglandins   Hormones that soften the cervix and stimulate the onset of uterine contractions.

Re-direct   The process of renewing direction-giving, before, during and after a given activity.

Relaxin   A hormone that softens ligaments and connective tissues during pregnancy, to facilitate birth.

SRM   Spontaneous rupture of the membranes surrounding the baby in the uterus.

Startle reflex   The automatic reaction to a stimulus perceived to be threatening, that produces an increase in tension in neck muscles and may spread elsewhere.

Syntometrine   A drug injected into the mother's thigh, usually just after the baby's first shoulder emerges, to speed up the delivery of the placenta.

Thinking-in-activity   The process of intelligently creating the best conditions for achieving our ends effectively and efficiently, including inhibition, non-doing and direction-sending.

Use of the self   The way we employ and coordinate our mind-body (our awareness, intentions and the body as a whole) in our everyday acts.

Index